FEMININE SINGULAR

Since earliest recorded history the unmarried woman has, apart from courtship for marriage, met with exploitation, frustration, ridicule, contempt and pity and, when her achievements surmounted these social denigrations, with astonished admiration.

Her story through the ages is told in these pages by extracts from the works of illustrious philosophers, writers and by contemporary comments. How men have regarded her is voiced by such authors as Shakespeare, Goldsmith, Charles Dickens, Bernard Shaw and T. S. Eliot. How single women have themselves thought and felt comes from the words of such famous writers as St. Teresa, Elizabeth I, Hannah More, Charlotte Brontë, Christina Rossetti and Katharine Whitehorn.

This selection, rich in contrast, literary excellence and wit, presents a piece of social history of remarkable authenticity.

FEMININE SINGULAR

Triumphs and Tribulations
of the
Single Woman

An Anthology

chosen by
The National Council for the Single Woman
and her Dependants

edited by
Roxane Arnold and Olive Chandler

A FEMINA BOOK

First published 1974 by Femina Books Ltd.

SBN: 85043 015 1

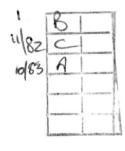

Distributed by Macdonald and Janes Publishers, St. Giles House, Poland Street, London W1
Typesetting by Stevenage Typesetters.
Printed and bound by The Garden City Press Ltd, Letchworth, Herts.

CONTENTS

ILLUSTRATIONS

FOREWORD

By Dame Flora Robson, D.B.E.
President, National Council for the Single Woman and her Dependants.

Everybody must know a woman whose life is sad because she is single. Some sink beneath the weight of enforced loneliness, others rise shining with courage above it. This is the stuff of which novels and films are made. We can all understand and sympathise and try to help. But what of women who are single from choice? What leads them to choose such a state deliberately? This book shows at least some of the reasons. It also dispels the popular image of the single woman as a spectre haunting the corridors of other people's lives.

Despite Freud and all that has followed, the 19th century idea that all women are basically family women is hard to eradicate. Indeed, many people still feel that women who prefer pursuits other than producing and nurturing families are somehow morally subnormal or socially irresponsible. Dedication to religion or to art, however, carry exemption from this blame. People do not expect to read about St. Teresa doing the shopping or washing children's nappies, nor would they have expected a great pianist like Myra Hess to deprive her listeners of joy because of domestic problems.

Nevertheless, the career-woman is suspect even if married - how *can* she keep her husband and family happy if she is out of the home all day, and even when she is at home has her mind on other things?

Bernard Shaw said in *Man and Superman*, "The true artist will let his wife starve, his children go barefoot, his mother drudge for his living at seventy, sooner than work at anything but his art." This maxim is true for the goose as well as the gander.

Sacrifice of self is a socially acceptable habit for artists of either sex - and sacrifice of others, as Shaw indicated, is acceptable for men. But for women the sacrifice of others to their own lives, artistic or not, is frowned on. Many women, indeed, seem to be built for self-immolation - and this leads us to those many who are neither famous, religious nor artistic, who nevertheless dedicate their lives to succouring others either professionally, such as nurses, or social workers, or privately such as those who care for invalid relatives or parentless children. The key to successful self-sacrifice, if such a phrase may be used, is that it looks like sacrifice outside, but inside, in the heart, it is a glow of love.

One woman who experienced this was our Founder, the Rev. Mary Webster. She interrupted her studies to care for the sick and seriously impaired her own health in carrying out essential duties. She did not sacrifice others - she and her deeply important work were sacrificed. But Mary Webster was ordained and lived to carry out her work. She would have been proud to sponsor this book about the single woman's success.

Times change, of course, and there are better opportunities today for the single woman to make a place for herself and others like her in the world than there were when Mary Webster was trying to complete her studies for ordination. But it is fascinating to look down the long avenue of the ages and see how this minority of women have seemed to themselves and others. Perhaps this anthology's most important achievement is to show, emphatically, that the single woman is not, after all, alone.

Flora Robson

September 1974

INTRODUCTION

By Baroness Seear
Chairman, National Council for the Single Woman and her Dependants.

Whether we like it or not, women are news. Yet another book requires an explanation.

This anthology does not speak for the entire female sex. It is limited to the minority of women who remain single. Always a small proportion of the total whole, the single woman has existed in all eras, in all societies and in all classes. In a few cases, she is revered or even glamorized. More often, she is used or scorned or pitied. To many people, her singleness is more important than her womanhood, and far more important than the simple fact that she is a person, like all others, regardless of sex or marital status. It is from the isolated fact of singleness that the stereotype has been born.

If this book does nothing else, it shatters this stereotype. The single woman is portrayed here in a variety of types and with the whole human range of weaknesses and strengths. And this variety, it is shown, existed in antiquity as it exists today.

Yet varied though they are, single women have frequently encountered problems which are peculiar to them, particularly where the family, rather than the individual, is seen as the basic unit in society. Where, in such societies, it is not possible for the single woman to support herself, she is inevitably cast in the role of family appendage, a burden or a burden-bearer as the case may be.

In these circumstances, it is not surprising that many of the extracts in this book relate to education. For many women for very many years, education has provided the only key to the escape route leading to an independent job, an independent income and an independent existence. And as this book shows, many women, in response to family needs and social expectations, have abandoned this independence so hardly won.

Since education has been of such cardinal importance to the

single woman, it is not difficult to explain the over-representation of educated women in this anthology. Until very recently, it has been a common criticism of the women's movement that it is overwhelmingly middle-class, championed by professional women but lacking popular support. At first sight this book might provide such critics with additional ammunition. But it is almost tautologous to say that the better educated and the better off can make themselves heard more easily than the under-educated and the hard-up. In the past, and still to some extent today, those whose need has been greatest could not commit their case to paper and so do not speak through these pages. But because the voice of the single woman, in this anthology and elsewhere, is frequently a middle-class voice, this in no way means that the middle-class woman speaks for herself alone. The problems cut across classes as they cut across centuries and cultures. This is well illustrated by the National Council for the Single Woman and her Dependants, the organisation which has sponsored this book, and which has attracted into membership women of all types of educational and social backgrounds, drawn together by shared needs.

Finally, this book has been prepared not only because the story of the single woman needed to be told but because in these extracts it has been told so well. Of course it is a book with a purpose: but it is also for your pleasure.

Nancy Seear

September 1974

ACKNOWLEDGMENTS

Thanks are given to the friends and supporters of the National Council for the Single Woman and her Dependants who sent in contributions and made suggestions, and in particular to Miss Margery Renyarde who first suggested the idea of this Anthology. The Editors have, with regret, had to leave out much fascinating material. Thanks also to Lady Gardiner and Mrs. Carolyn Whitaker of Femina Books for their enthusiastic help, and to the unique Fawcett Library.

Acknowledgment is made to the following for permission to use extracts and selections from the works, speeches, poems, and illustrations listed below:—

George Allen & Unwin Ltd. - *Rapiers and Battleaxes* by Josephine Kamm.

Edward Arnold (Publishers) Ltd. - *Memoir of Anne Jemima Clough* by Blanche Athena Clough.

Barry & Jenkins - *The Woman's Side* by Clemence Dane.

G. Bell & Sons Ltd. - *The Cause* by Ray Strachey, including *Cassandra* by Florence Nightingale in Appendix I.

Ernest Benn Ltd. - *Earlier Letters of Gertrude Bell* edited by Elsa Richmond, published by Benn Bros. Ltd., London, 1937.

Ernest Benn Ltd. and A. P. Watt & Son (for late Sir Alan Herbert, C.H.) - poems by Sir Alan Herbert.

Adam and Charles Black - *From One Century to Another* by Elizabeth Haldane.

The British Council and Longman Group Ltd. - *The English-woman* by Cicely Hamilton 1940.

Cambridge University Press - *Elizabeth and the English*

Reformation by William P. Haugaard, *Hannah More* by M.G. Jones

Cambridge University Press and Professor M.M. Postan (Executor) - *Medieval English Nunneries* by Eileen Power.

Cassell & Co. Ltd. - *What Fools We Women Be* by Ellen Dorothy Abb.

Centaur Press Ltd. - *Pastel for Eliza* by Marjorie S. Broughall.

Chapman & Hall - *Marriage as a Trade* by Cicely Hamilton.

The Clarendon Press, Oxford - *Degrees by Degrees* by Annie M.A.H. Rogers.

Constable & Co. Ltd. - *Emily Davies and Girton College* by Barbara Stephen, *Florence Nightingale* by Mrs. Cecil Woodham-Smith, *Octavia Hill* by E. Moberly Bell.

The Controller Of Her Majesty's Stationery Office - *House of Commons Parliamentary Debates: Standing Committee H 26th May 1971.*

Daily Mail, London - article

Daily Telegraph - article.

The Literary Trustees Of Walter De La Mare and The Society Of Authors As Their Representative - *Miss Loo* by Walter de la Mare.

J.M. Dent & Sons Ltd. - *The Paston Letters* published by Everyman's Library Series.

Doubleday & Co. Inc. - *Lysistrata* by Aristophanes, translated by Benjamin Bickley Rogers, edited by Andrew Chiappe, published by Doubleday Anchor Books 1955.

Gerald Duckworth & Co. Ltd. - poem by Hilaire Belloc.

Faber & Faber Ltd. - *Collected Poems 1909-62,* and *The Cocktail Party* by T.S. Eliot.

The Guardian - articles.

Robert Hale Ltd. - *Parson's Daughter* by Esylt Newbery.

David Higham Associates Ltd. - *Roman Women* by J.P.V.D. Balsdon, published by The Bodley Head 1962.

Hodder & Stoughton Ltd. - *In Quest of a Kingdom* by Leslie D. Weatherhead.

The Hogarth Press and The Literary Estate Of Virginia Woolf - *Three Guineas.*

Hutchinson Publishing Group Ltd. - *Unshackled* by Dame Christabel Pankhurst.

Mrs. Enid Huws Jones - *Margery Fry, The Essential Amateur.*

Mrs. Josephine Kamm - *How Different from Us* and *Hope Deferred.*

Macmillan, London & Basingstoke - poem *"The Old Ladies"* by Colin Ellis from *Mournful Numbers,* and *Testament of Friendship* by Vera Brittain.

The Mansell Collection - photograph of Florence Nightingale.

Mrs. Rosalind Messenger - *The Doors of Opportunity.*

The Methodist Publishing House - *Child Care Pioneers* by Margaret Weddell.

Methuen & Co. Ltd. - *Sister Dora* by Jo Manton, and poem by Harry Graham.

Methuen & Co. Ltd. and Miss Clare Campbell (Literary Executrix) - *Mary Kingsley* by Olwen Campbell.

National Museum Of Italy, Rome - *Statue of Chief Vestal Virgin.*

National Portrait Gallery - *Queen Elizabeth I* by unknown artist, and *Octavia Hill* by Sargent.

The Observer - article.

Oxford University Press - *The Lady's Not For Burning* by Christopher Fry.

Oxford And Cambridge University Presses - *New English Bible,* Second Edition 1970.

Dr. Richard Pankhurst - photograph of Christabel Pankhurst.

Paulist/Newman Press - *The Letters of St. Jerome* translated by Charles Christopher Mierov, published by The Newman Press and Longmans, Green & Co. 1963.

Estate Of Late John Cowper Powys and Jonathan Cape Ltd. - *The Meaning of Culture* by John Cowper Powys.

Punch - cartoons and extract.

Miss Kathleen Richardson - translations from Geoffrey Chaucer.

Routledge & Kegan Paul Ltd. - *The Incense Tree* by Diana Hopkinson, and *A Suppressed Cry* by Victoria Glendinning.

Sands & Co. Publishers - *The Way of Perfection* by St. Teresa of Avila, translated by a discalced Carmelite.

Search Press Ltd. - *Ancrene Riwle,* Search Press 1971.

Martin Secker & Warburg – *The Life and Death of Harriet Martineau* by Vera Wheatley.

The Society Of Authors On Behalf Of The Bernard Shaw Estate - *Saint Joan,* and *The Adventures of the Black Girl in her Search for God.*

The Society Of Authors and Miss Rosamund Lehmann - *Invitation to the Waltz* by Rosamund Lehmann.

Baroness Stocks - *Eleanor Rathbone.*
Baroness Summerskill - *A Woman's World.*
The Times - various articles.
Nicolette Milnes-Walker - *When I put out to Sea.*

For the very few instances where our searches have failed to find the holders of copyright we offer our apologies.

Roxane Arnold, Director, National Council for the Single
Woman and her Dependants.

Olive Chandler.
Editors

APÉRITIF

SOCRATES, 470 - 399 BC

Whether you marry or not, you will live to regret it.

ST. JEROME, 340 - 420

It is not disparaging marriage when virginity is preferred to it. No one compares evil with good. Let married women glory too, since they come second to virgins. "Increase", He says, "and multiply and fill the earth". Let him who is to fill the earth increase and multiply. Your company is in heaven.

MICHEL DE MONTAIGNE, 1533 - 1592

It (marriage) happens as with cages: the birds outside despair of getting in, and likewise those within despair of getting out.

* * *

1

1

THE BIBLE

THE OLD TESTAMENT

GENESIS c 1860 BC

Abraham's servant is sent to seek a wife for Isaac and is guided to Rebecca
The girl was very beautiful, a virgin, who had had no intercourse with a man.

The servant talks with her family
I saw Rebecca coming out with her water-jar on her shoulder ... I blessed the Lord, the God of my master Abraham, who had led me by the right road to take my master's niece for his son ... Laban and Bethuel answered, "This is from the Lord; we can say nothing for or against. Here is Rebecca herself; take her and go. She shall be the wife of your master's son, as the Lord has decreed."

THE BOOK OF JUDGES, c 1143 BC

"She went with her companions and mourned her virginity"
Jephthah made this vow to the Lord: 'If thou wilt deliver the Ammonites into my hands, then the first creature that comes out of the door of my house to meet me when I return from them in peace shall be the Lord's; I will offer that as a whole-offering.' So Jephthah crossed over to attack the Ammonites, and the Lord delivered them into his hands. He routed them with great slaughter all the way from Aroer to

Minnith, taking twenty towns and as far as Abel-keramim. Thus Israel crushed Ammon. But when Jephthah came to his house in Mizpah, who should come out to meet him with tambourines and dances but his daughter, and she his only child; he had no other, neither son nor daughter. When he saw her, he rent his clothes and said, 'Alas, my daughter, you have broken my heart, such trouble you have brought upon me. I have made a vow to the Lord and I cannot go back.' She replied, 'Father, you have made a vow to the Lord; do to me what you have solemnly vowed, since the Lord has avenged you on the Ammonites, your enemies. But, father, grant me this one favour. For two months let me be, that I may roam the hills with my companions and mourn that I must die a virgin.' 'Go', he said, and he let her depart for two months. She went with her companions and mourned her virginity on the hills. At the end of two months she came back to her father, and he fulfilled the vow he had made; she died a virgin. It became a tradition that the daughters of Israel should go year by year and commemorate the fate of Jephthah's daughter, four days in every year.

THE FIRST BOOK OF KINGS, c 1015 BC

"She took care of the King"
King David was now a very old man and, though they wrapped clothes round him, he could not keep warm. So his household said to him, 'Let us find a young virgin for your majesty, to attend you and take care of you; and let her lie in your bosom, sir, and make you warm.' So they searched all over Israel for a beautiful maiden and found Abishag, a Shunammite, and brought her to the king. She was a very beautiful girl, and she took care of the king and waited on him, but he had no intercourse with her.

*   *   *

THE NEW TESTAMENT

THE GOSPEL ACCORDING TO LUKE, AD32

"Distracted by her many tasks"
While they were on their way Jesus came to a village where a woman named Martha made him welcome in her home. She had a sister, Mary, who seated herself at the Lord's feet and stayed there listening to his words. Now Martha was distracted by her many tasks, so she came to him and said, "Lord, do you not care that my sister has left me to get on with the work by myself? Tell her to come and lend a hand." But the Lord answered, "Martha, Martha, you are fretting and fussing about so many things; but one thing is necessary. The part that Mary has chosen is best; and it shall not be taken away from her."

THE FIRST EPISTLE OF PAUL THE APOSTLE TO THE CORINTHIANS, AD59

The unmarried woman careth for the things of the Lord, that she may be holy in body and in spirit.

*   *   *

2

ANTIQUITY

EGYPT

HERODOTUS OF HALICARNASSUS, 484 - 424 BC

The History of Herodotus, c 450 - 430 BC
Translated by George Rawlinson, 1858

Sons need not support their parents unless they choose, but daughters must, whether they choose or no.

The swineherds, notwithstanding that they are of pure Egyptian blood, are forbidden to enter into any of the temples, which are open to all other Egyptians; and further, no one will give his daughter in marriage to a swineherd, or take a wife from among them, so that the swineherds are forced to intermarry among themselves.

SOCRATES SURNAMED SCHOLASTICUS, c 379 - c 445 AD

The Ecclesiastical History of Socrates surnamed Scholasticus, or the Advocate, 305 - 445 AD

Of Hypatia the Female Philosopher, 414 AD
There was a woman at Alexandria named Hypatia, daughter of the philosopher Theon, who made such attainments in

5

literature and science, as to far surpass all the philosophers of her own time. Having succeeded to the school of Plato and Photinus, she explained the principles of philosophy to her auditors, many of whom came from a distance to receive her instructions. Such was her self-possession and ease of manner, arising from the refinement and cultivation of her mind, that she not infrequently appeared in public in presence of the magistrates, without ever losing in an assembly of men that dignified modesty of deportment for which she was conspicuous, and which gained for her universal respect and admiration. Yet even she fell a victim to the political jealousy which at that time prevailed. For as she had frequent interviews with Orestes, it was calumniously reported among the Christian populace, that it was by her influence he was prevented from being reconciled to Cyril. Some of them therefore, whose ringleader was a reader named Peter, hurried away by a fierce and bigoted zeal, entered into a conspiracy against her; and observing her as she returned home in her carriage, they dragged her from it, and carried her to the church called Caesareum, where they completely stripped her, and then murdered her with shells. After tearing her body in pieces, they took her mangled limbs to a place called Cinaron, and there burnt them. An act so inhuman could not fail to bring the greatest opprobrium, not only upon Cyril, but also upon the whole Alexandrian Church. And surely nothing can be further from the spirit of Christianity than the allowance of massacres, fights, and transactions of that sort. This happened in the month of March during Lent, in the fourth year of Cyril's episcopate, under the tenth consulate of Honorius, and the sixth of Theodosius.

GREECE

ARISTOPHANES, c 450 - 388 BC

Lysistrata, 411 BC
Translated by B. B. Rogers 1878

"Sit as we may with our spells and our auguries"
Magistrate. Men, I suppose, have their youth everlastingly.
Lysistrata. Nay, but it isn't the same with a man:
Grey though he be when he comes from the battlefield,
Still if he wishes to marry, he can.
Brief is the spring and the flower of our womanhood,
Once let it slip, and it comes not again;
Sit as we may with our spells and our auguries,
Never a husband will marry us then.

*   *   *

ROME

J. P. V. D. BALSDON

Roman Women, 1962

Vestal Virgin

The election of a Vestal Virgin was not an everyday affair; it happened no more frequently on an average than once in every five years. Twenty candidates — girls between six and ten years old, both of whose parents must be living — were selected by the Pontifex Maximus, and from these one was chosen by lot. Under the Republic daughters of the noblest families alone were eligible, at first only patricians. There was no dearth of candidates in the early and middle republic; but times changed, and Augustus lowered the social qualification greatly when in AD5 he was forced to admit the daughters of freedmen as candidates.

At the dramatic moment when the lot had made its choice, the child was 'taken' by the Pontifex Maximus who addressed her as 'Amata' and pronounced the traditional formula for admission to the Order. Immediately she passed out of her father's control *(patria potestas)*, and indeed right out of her family; after this she would not count as one of the next of kin if even her closest blood-relative died intestate; nor, if she herself died intestate, did her property pass to her blood-relations. It went, instead, to the State. But she could make a will, for she acquired legal independence on becoming a Vestal Virgin; and, indeed, she became from the start a young woman of property. For she was given money — the equivalent perhaps of a dowry — at the start. By the time of the early Empire this sum, voted by the Senate, might be as large as two million sesterces, twice the amount of a rich girl's normal dowry; and there was even a case where an unsuccessful candidate was given a million sesterces. If candidates no longer came forward willingly, it was necessary to attract them by bribes. This is a not unfamiliar principle of public economy.

So, with little understanding of the trials and temptations which lay ahead, the child was committed to thirty years of virginity. . . .

We have an account of a banquet at which on August 24th, 69 BC, four Vestal Virgins were present — the four seniors, it may be assumed, while the two juniors, like a pair of Cinderellas, stayed at home to look after the fire. The dinner celebrated the installation by an augur of a new Flamen Martialis. The pontiffs occupied two tables, the ladies (who included the wife of the new Flamen and his mother-in-law) occupied a third. The menu is preserved too; and by comparison the banquet of the most apolaustic of City Companies would appear to be a frugal meal. Its thirty dishes included asparagus, oysters (as many as anyone could eat) and delicious *pâtés* of all kinds.

Vestal Virgins travelled through the streets of Rome in carriages at public festivals. They were attended in public by a lictor. When they gave evidence in court, they were exempted, together with the Flamen Dialis, from the necessity of taking an oath. They could annul the death sentence of a prisoner

8

whom they encountered, as long as it was by accident, on his way to execution. And under Augustus and his successors they not only attended the theatre, but sat there in privileged seats, where they were joined by the ladies of the imperial house. And when the greatest of these imperial ladies, the widow of Augustus, was consecrated, they were made responsible for her cult.

Their public importance, especially at moments of crisis, was indisputable. It was through the senior Vestal Virgin that the Empress Messalina in her last desperation sought to influence Claudius. And when in AD 69 Vitellius hoped to arrest for a moment the march of the victorious Flavian army on Rome, the Vestal Virgins carried his letter to the Flavian commander. Their sacrosanctity gave the security of a strong room; and so they guarded important documents, the wills of leading statesmen, for instance, and even the wills of emperors, who were themselves High Priests.

What of their relation with men — who, as a sex, were allowed to enter the Atrium by day, but never by night?

The purity of the Vestal Virgins was the token and guarantee of the good health and salvation of Rome itself; how often, knowing this, they must have prayed to Vesta that they might not succumb to temptation . . .

Whereas if a Vestal Virgin was found to have let the sacred fire go out, she suffered nothing worse than a thrashing by the Pontifex Maximus, if she was found guilty of sexual immorality, the partner in her guilt was flogged to death — like a slave, *sub furca* — in the Comitium and she was immured alive in an underground chamber under the Campus Sceleratus by the Colline Cate. If, by contrast, a *bona fide* secular virgin was doomed to death by strangulation — like the young daughter of Sejanus, who was supposedly implicated in her father's scheming in AD 31 — she was debauched by her executioner when the rope was already around her neck, because it was inauspicious to execute a virgin.

Plutarch gives this grim description of the erring Vestal Virgin's doom:

'A small underground chamber is constructed with access from above by a ladder. It contains a bed, a lighted lamp and small portions of the bare necessities of existence — bread, water in a jar, milk and oil; so that the Romans may feel easy in their consciences and nobody can say that by starvation they have murdered a woman consecrated by the most sacred ritual.

Inside a litter enclosed by curtains, bound and gagged so that her voice may not be heard, they carry the victim through the Forum. People make way without a word, and escort the procession in utter silence and deep dejection. There is no spectacle in the world more terrifying and in Rome no day of comparable horror.

When the cortège reaches the end of its journey, the attendants undo the bonds and, after he has prayed in silence, stretching out his hands to the gods to explain the necessity of his act, the Pontifex Maximus takes her by the hand, a thick cloak hiding her face, and sets her on the ladder. He and the rest of the Pontiffs turn away while she descends the ladder. Then the ladder is pulled up and the entry to the chamber closed and covered with deep earth level with the surrounding ground.'

This was not, obviously, an everyday happening in Rome. Indeed, there are less than ten occasions in the whole of Roman history when this punishment is known to have been exacted.

3

THE DARK AGES

JOSEPHINE KAMM

Hope Deferred, 1965

St. Hild, 614 - 680

By far the most outstanding of the scholarly women was St. Hilda (or Hild), whose influence on affairs was infinitely greater than the influence any woman could exert during the Middle Ages. Hild, who was born in 614, was a member of the royal family of Northumbria, her father Hereric being nephew to the king. According to Bede, Hild's mother had a prophetic dream shortly before the birth of her child. She dreamed that she was searching for her husband but could not find him; 'but, after having used all her industry to seek him, she found a most precious jewel under her garment, which, whilst she was looking on it very attentively, cast such a light as spread itself throughout Britain'.

The first part of the prophecy, says Bede, was fulfilled when Hereric was murdered. The child Hild was then adopted by her great-uncle Edwin and his wife Ethelburga, a Christian who, under the guidance of Paulinus, was trying to convert the Northumbrians. Paulinus converted Hild when she was twelve or thirteen; and she was baptized, together with her great-uncle and his nobles, at an impressive ceremony in York.

In these turbulent times pagan imposters and rulers checked the spread of Christianity, which lost ground after Edwin had been killed. But when Bishop Aidan was sent to evangelize the area Hild came directly under his influence, and at the age of thirty-three she decided to become a nun. She intended to join her sister, a nun in the convent of Chelles near Paris, and had journeyed as far as East Anglia when Aidan, who saw in her the ideal religious leader, recalled her to Northumbria. He gave her a small estate on the banks of the river Wear, and she lived for a year in this deserted spot in a tiny convent in the company of a small band of dedicated women. Aidan then made her abbess of a double monastery at Hartlepool; and there, Hild, 'the servant of Christ, being set over that monastery, began immediately to reduce all things to a regular system, according as she had been instructed by learned men; for Bishop Aidan, and other religious men that knew her and loved her, frequently visited and diligently instructed her, because of her innate wisdom and inclination to the service of God'.

Hild's prestige was immensely increased when a Christian king of Northumbria placed his one-year-old daughter Aelflaed in her care, giving her a dower of twelve hides (estates) of land. Under Hild's protection the child was reared in convent ways and discipline and lived to succeed her as abbess. Aelflaed's reputation as superior was high, for Eddi, the biographer of St. Wilfrid, wrote approvingly of her as the adviser of the entire province.

Aelflaed was malleable, but many of the girls who came to Hild as novices were wild and untutored and found monastic life impossibly rigorous. In order to break them in as gently as possible Hild arranged a special system of instruction for the newly converted women and kept them in a separate part of the women's building until she judged them ready to join the rest of the community. Her rule may have been strict, but she was just and humane, and her nuns loved her dearly.

The king's daughter was still a small child when Hild was transferred once more, and she accompanied the abbess, who was supervising the building of her new abbey Streaneshalch, which was renamed Whitby by the Danes.

Under Hild's rule Whitby became the most famous of the monasteries in the north-east of England. 'Hild's prudence was so great,' said Bede, 'that not only indifferent persons, but even kings and princes, as occasion offered, asked and received her advice; she obliged those who were under her direction to attend so much to reading of the Holy Scriptures, and to exercise themselves so much in works of justice, that many might be there found fit for ecclesiastical duties, and to serve at the altar.' Five of her monks afterwards became bishops, the best known being St. John of Beverley.

Hild was also credited with miracles; she was said, for instance, to turn snakes into stones, and to receive homage from wild geese. And it was under her influence that the untutored herdsman Caedmon wrote his verses. When she heard him recite the words which had been spoken to him in a dream, Hild with her monks translated some passages from the Scriptures from Latin into Old English which she asked Caedmon to turn into verse. She was so moved by his poetry and his piety that she accepted him as a monk, and he spent the rest of his life turning passages from the Scriptures into his own brand of verse.

To Hild, all men from the herdsman to the nobly born were equal; and she was held in such affectionate respect that 'all that knew her called (her) Mother'. She died at the age of sixty-five. In the last year of her life she had founded a small monastery at Hackness; and at the moment of her death one of the Hackness nuns is said to have had a vision of a strong light in which she saw the abbess being conducted to heaven by angels.

After the death of Hild and her successor Aelflaed, the influence of Whitby declined; but in the south of England little groups of scholarly nuns were keeping alive the spirit of learning.

One of these groups was centred on the convent of Barking, founded by Earconwald for his sister Ethelburga . . . Ethelburga, a saintly woman, died about 676 and Hildelith succeeded her . . .

The new abbess was a keen scholar . . . She administered the monastery for a considerable time; and under her rule Barking became, and remained for many years, an influential centre of learning . . .

If there was no schooling in the modern sense of the word, learning was spread from one religious settlement to another.

THE ANCRENE RIWLE
THE ANCHORESSES' RULE c 1230

Translated into modern English by M. B. Salu, 1955

Let no one deceive herself into thinking that she can treat herself gently. She will not for the life of her be able to keep herself pure and strictly maintain her chastity without two things, as St. Ailred the abbot wrote to his sister. The one is mortification of the flesh by fasts, vigils, disciplines, harsh garments, a hard bed, the enduring of sickness and the performance of heavy labours. The other is the virtues of the heart, devotion, compassion, love well-directed, humility, and other such virtues . . .

Unless need compels you, my dear sister, and your director advises it, you must not keep any animal except a cat. An anchoress who keeps animals looks more like a housewife, as Martha was, and cannot easily have peace of heart and be Mary, Martha's sister; for in such a case she has to think of the cow's fodder and the herdsman's wages, say nice things to the hayward, call him names when he impounds the cow, and yet pay damages nonetheless! It is odious, Christ knows, when there are complaints in a village about the anchoress's animals. Now if someone must needs keep one, let her see to it that it does not annoy anyone or do any harm to anybody, and that her thoughts are not taken up with it. An anchoress ought not to have anything which draws her heart outward.

4

THE MIDDLE AGES

C. M. ANTONY

St. Catherine of Siena. Her Life and Times, 1915

St. Catherine, 1347 - 1380

While Knowledge shines forth in St. Dominic, Wisdom in St. Thomas, and Counsel in St. Antoninus, Almighty God chose a woman to personify, as a Saint of the Order, the special Gift of Understanding.
From this gift flowed St. Catherine's whole spiritual philosophy. She was naturally, as we have said, an optimist. "Is not sadness the worst of all sins?" she was to write, a few years later, to Neri di Landoccio, whose supersensitive nature was too deeply tinged with melancholy. But Catherine's extreme cheerfulness was by no means merely natural. It was founded on the idea that God demands of us, not absolute, but attempted Perfection; that He does not require of the soul entirely to eradicate a single fault, but to attempt to eradicate it with all its powers. "God does not ask a perfect work, but infinite desire". Consequently there can be no discouragement, even for those naturally pessimistic. For all God asks is that each should do his best.

*   *   *

EILEEN POWER, 1889 - 1940

Medieval English Nunneries 1275 - 1535, published 1922

"The refuge of the gently born"

It has been shown that the proportion of women who became nuns was very small in comparison with the total female population. It has indeed been insufficiently recognised that the medieval nunneries were recruited almost entirely from among the upper classes. They were essentially aristocratic institutions, the refuge of the gently born. At Romsey Abbey a list of 91 sisters at the election of an abbess in 1333 is full of well-known county names. The names of Bassett, Sackville, Covert, Hussey, Tawke and Farnfold occur at Easebourne; Lewknor, St. John, Okehurst, Michelgrove and Sidney at Rusper, the two small and poor nunneries in Sussex. The return of the subsidy in 1377 enumerates the sisters of Minchin Barrow and, as their historian points out, "among the family names of these ladies are some of the best that the western counties could produce". The other Somerset houses were equally aristocratic, and an examination of the roll of prioresses for almost any medieval convent in any part of England will give the same result, even in the smallest and poorest nunneries, the inmates of which were reduced to begging alms. These ladies appear sometimes to have had the spirit of their race, as they often had its manners and its tastes. For 21 years Isabel Stanley, Prioress of King's Mead, Derby, refused to pay a rent due from her house to the Abbot of Burton; at last the Abbot sent his bailiff to distrain for it and she spoke her mind in good set terms. "Wenes these churles to overlede me," cried this worthy daughter of a knightly family, "or sue the lawe agayne me? They shall not be so hardy but they shall avye upon their bodies and be nailed with arrows; for I am a gentlewoman, comen of the greatest of Lancashire and Cheshire, and that they shall know right well". A tacit recognition of the aristocratic character of the convents is to be found in the fact that bishops were often at pains to mention the good birth of the girls whom, in accordance with a general right, they nominated to certain houses on certain occasions. Thus Wykeham wrote to the Abbess of St. Mary's Winchester, bidding her admit Joan Bleden, "quest de bone et

16

honeste condition, come nous sumes enformes". More frequently still the candidates were described as '"domicella" or "damoysele". At least one instance is extant of a bishop ordering that all the nuns of a house were to be of noble condition.

"The poor labourer upon the land had no need to get rid of his daughter"

The fact that the greater portion of the female population was unaffected by the existence of the outlet provided by conventual life for women's energies is a significant one. The reason for it — paradoxical as this may sound — lies in the very narrowness of the sphere to which women of gentle birth were confined. The disadvantage of rank is that so many honest occupations are not, in its eyes, honourable occupations. In the lowest ranks of society the poor labourer upon the land had no need to get rid of his daughter, if he could not find her a husband, nor would it have been to his interest to do so; for, working in the fields among his sons, or spinning and brewing with his wife at home, she could earn a supplementary if not a living wage. The tradesman or artisan in the town was in a similar position. He recognised that the ideal course was to find a husband for his growing girl, but the alternative was in no sense that she should eat out her heart and his income during long years at home; and if he were too poor to provide her with a sufficient dower, he could and often did apprentice her to a trade. The number of industries which were carried on by women in the middle ages shows that for the burgess and lower classes there were other outlets besides marriage; and then, as now, domestic service provided for many. But the case of the well-born lady was different. The knight or the county gentleman could not apprentice his superfluous daughters to a pursemaker or a weaver in the town; not from them were drawn the regrateresses in the market place and the harvest gatherers in the field; nor was it theirs to make the parti-coloured bed and shake the coverlet, worked with grapes and unicorns, in some rich vintner's house. There remained for him, if he did not wish or could not afford to keep them at home and for them, if they desired some scope for their young energies, only marriage or else a convent, where they might go with a smaller dower than a husband of their own rank would demand.

CHRISTOPHER FRY

The Lady's not for Burning, 1949

Time: 1400 either more or less or exactly

Alizon: I am quite usual, with five elder sisters. My birth
Was a great surprise to my parents, I think. There had been
A misunderstanding and I appeared overnight
As mushrooms do. It gave my father thrombosis.
He thought he would never be able to find enough husbands
For six of us, and so he made up his mind
To simplify matters and let me marry God.
He gave me to a convent.

EILEEN POWER

Margaret de Prestewych released from observance 1383

The case of Margaret de Prestewych has been preserved in the
register of Robert de Stretton, Bishop of Coventry and
Lichfield; and it is satisfactory to know that one energetic girl
at least succeeded in making good her protests and in
escaping from her prison. In her eighth year or thereabouts,
according to her own petition to the Pope, her friends
compelled her against her will to enter the priory of the nuns
of Seton, of the order of St. Augustine, and take on her the
habit of a novice. She remained there, as in a prison, for
several years, always protesting that she had never made nor
ever would willingly make any profession. And then, seeing
that she must by profession be excluded from her inheritance,
she feigned herself sick and took to her bed. But this did not
prevent her being carried to the church at the instance of her
rivals and blessed by a monk, in spite of her cries and protests
that she would not remain in that priory or in any other order.
On the first opportunity she went forth from the priory
without leave and returned to the world, which in heart she
had never left, and married Robert de Holand, publicly after

18

banns, and had issue. The bishop, to whom the case had been referred by the Pope, found upon inquiry that these things were true, and in 1383 released her from the observance of her order.

*   *   *

GEORGE BERNARD SHAW, 1856 - 1950

St. Joan, 1923

Joan of Arc, born 1412, burnt 1431

Joan: I come from the land and have gotten my strength working on the land . . . I shall dare, dare and dare again, in God's name! . . . A man . . . took an action against me for breach of promise but I never promised him. I am a soldier; I do not want to be thought of as a woman. I will not dress as a woman. I do not care for the things women care for. They dream of lovers and of money. I dream of leading a charge and of placing the big guns . . . my heart is full of courage, not of anger . . . I am not proud. I never speak unless I know I am right. . . .

Dunois: I see that some day she will go ahead when she has only ten men to do the work of a hundred . . .

Joan: I am not proud and disobedient, I am a poor girl, and so ignorant that I do not know A from B . . .

The Inquisitor: The devilish pride that has led her into her present peril has left no mark on her countenance . . . it has even left no mark on her character outside those special matters in which she is so proud; so that you will see a diabolical pride and a natural humility seated side by side in the selfsame soul . . .

Joan: There is great wisdom in the simplicity of a beast and sometimes great foolishness in the wisdom of scholars . . . I cannot write . . . I can make my mark . . .

Light your fire . . . do you think I dread it as much as the life of a rat in a hole? . . .

To shut me from the light of the sky and the sight of the fields and flowers. To chain my feet so that I can never ride again . . . nor climb the hills; to make me breathe foul damp darkness

19

and to keep from me everything that brings me back to the love of God . . . All this is worse than the furnace in the Bible that was heated seven times. I could do without my warhorse; I could drag about in a skirt: I could let the banners and the trumpets and the knights and soldiers pass me and leave me behind as they leave other women; if only I could still hear the wind in the trees, the larks in the sunshine, the young lambs crying through the healthy frost, and the blessed, blessed Church bells that send my angel voices floating to me on the wind. But without these things I cannot live....

CHRISTOPHER FRY

The Lady's not for Burning, 1949

Time: 1400 either more or less or exactly

> *Jennet:* Why do they call me a witch?
> Remember my father was an alchemist.
> I live alone, preferring loneliness
> To the companionable suffocation of an aunt.
> I still amuse myself with simple experiments
> In my father's laboratory. Also I speak
> French to my poodle. Then you must know
> I have a peacock which on Sundays
> Dines with me indoors. Not long ago
> A new little serving maid carrying the food
> Heard its cry, dropped everything and ran,
> Never to come back, and told all whom she met
> That the Devil was dining with me.

GEOFFREY CHAUCER, c 1340 - 1400

The Clerk's Tale of Patient Griselda, c 1379

Translated into modern English by Kathleen Richardson

A little distance from a palace fair
Whose noble lord was planning to be wed,
There was a village, sited charmingly,
In which the poor folk of the neighbourhood
Pastured their beasts, and made their lowly homes,
And gained a living through their thrifty toil,
Tilling the soil that yielded crops and fruits.

Among these poorer folk there dwelt a man
Was held to be poorest of them all.
A daughter had he, beautiful to see;
Griselda was the name of this young girl,
And both for beauty and for virtue known,
She was the fairest maid in all the world.
Though nurtured in a poor and lowly home
There was no hint of sinful thought in her.
More often of the well than of the wine
She drank, and her all virtuous thoughts did please;
She knew hard labour, but not idle ease.

Although this maiden was of tender age,
Yet in the breast of her virginity
There was enclosed a soul mature and staid,
And with great reverence, and in charity,
She for her father cared most tenderly.
Some sheep she kept, and watched them while she span;
And on her walks she gathered useful herbs
That served as food for both of them each day.
She ever put her father's welfare first
And to him showed obedience, and great love.

21

The Physician's Tale c 1386 - 1391

Translated into modern English by Kathleen Richardson

"Blessed be God that I shall die a maid".
    So when this worthy knight, Virginius,
    Through sentence of the justice, Apius,
    Was forced his dearest daughter now to give
    Unto the judge, in lechery to live,
    Homeward he went, and seated in his hall
    He straightway did his daughter to him call;
    And with a face distraught, and ashen cold,
    Her humble countenance did he behold,
    With father's pity striking through his heart;
    But from his purpose would he not depart.

    "Daughter", quoth he, "Virginia - true to name -
    There are two ways, either by death or shame,
    That thou must suffer; woeful is my state!
    For never didst thou merit such a fate
    To perish with a sword, or with a knife.
    O my dear daughter, ender of my life,
    Whom I have loved with such affection kind
    That thou wast ever in my heart enshrined;
    O daughter, thou the cause of my last woe.
    And of my life my latest joy also,
    O gem of chastity, in mild patience
    Accept thy death, for this is my sentence.
    For love and not for hate, thou hast to die.
    My hand must cause thy death, most piteously.
    Alas! that ever Apius did thee see!
    For this his falseness hath condemned thee!"
    And thereon he recounted, what before
    Ye all have heard; no need to tell it more.

    "O mercy, my dear father!" quoth this maid.
    And saying thuswise, both her arms she laid
    About his neck, as she was wont to do;
    And tears of sorrow did her cheeks bedew
    As thus she spake: "Good father, must I die?
    Is there no grace? Is there no remedy?"
    "None, my dear daughter", sadly answered he.

"Then give me respite, father mine", quoth she,
"That I may mourn my fate a little space;
For Jephthah granted to his daughter grace
And time to grieve, before his child he slew.
God knows full well, no evil did she do,
Only right joyously had hastened she
To welcome him with great solemnity".
And with those words she fell into a swoon;
But after coming to herself full soon,
She raised herself, and to her father said,
"Blessed be God that I shall die a maid!
Put me to death before I die of shame.
Do with your child your will, in God's great name!"

And saying thus, she begged in her distress
That with his sword he strike with carefulness;
And swooned again, as fearful to depart.
Her father then, with a full sorrowful heart,
Smote off her head, and held it by the hair.
And hastened to present it, then and there,
Unto the judge, where he did sit in court.

*   *   *

THE PASTON LETTERS

*Written by Various Persons of Rank or Consequence during
the Reigns of Henry VI, Edward IV, Richard III and
Henry VII, 1422 - 1509*

Elizabeth Clere to her cousin, John Paston, 29th of June, 1454

To my cousin, John Paston, be this letter delivered.
Trusty and well-beloved cousin, I commend me to you,
desiring to hear of your welfare and good speed in your
matters, the which I pray God send you to his plesaunce and
to your heart's ease.
Cousin, I let you weet that Scroope hath been in this country
to see my cousin your sister, and he hath spoken with my
cousin your mother, and she desireth of him that he should
show you the indentures made between the knight that hath

his daughter and him, whether that Scroope, if he were married and fortuned to have children, if those children should inherit his land, or his daughter, the which is married.

Cousin, for this cause take good heed to his indentures, for he is glad to show you them, or whom ye will assign with you; and he saith to me he is the last in the tayle of his livelihood the which is three hundred and fifty marks *(233l. 6s. 8d.)* and better, as Watkin Shipdam saith, for he hath taken a compt of his livelihood divers times; and Scroope saith to me if he be married and have a son and heir, his daughter that is married shall have of his livelihood fifty marks *(33l. 6s. 8d.)* and no more; and therefore, cousin, meseemeth he were good for my cousin your sister with that ye might get her a better; and if ye can get a better I would advise you to labour it in as short time as ye may goodly, for she was never in so great sorrow as she is now-a-days, for she may not speak with no man, whosoever come, ne not may see nor speak with my man, nor with servants of her mother's, but that she beareth her an hand otherwise than she meaneth; and she hath since Easter the most part been beaten once in the week or twice, and sometimes twice on a day, and her head broken in two or three places. Wherefore, cousin, she hath sent to me by Fryar Newton in great counsel, and prayeth me that I would send to you a letter of her heaviness, and pray you to be her good brother, as her trust is in you; and she saith if ye may see by his evidences that his children and hers may inherit, and she to have reasonable jointure, she hath heard so much of his birth and his conditions, that and ye will she will have him, whether that her mother will or will not, notwithstanding it is told her his person is simple, for she saith men shall have the more dainty *(deyute)* of her, if she rule her to him as she ought to do.

Cousin, it is told me there is a goodly man in your inn, of the which the father died lately, and if ye think that he were better for her than Scroope, it would be laboured, and give Scroope a goodly answer, that he be not put off till ye be sure of a better; for he said when he was with me but if he have some comfortable answer of you he will no more labour in this matter, because he might not see my cousin your sister, and he saith he might have seen her and she had been better than she is; and that causeth him to deem that her mother was not well willing; and so have I sent my cousin your mother word;

24

wherefore, cousin, think on this matter, for sorrow oftentime causeth women to beset them otherwise than they should do, and if she were in that case, I wot well ye would be sorry: cousin, I pray you burn this letter, that your men nor none other men see it; for and my cousin your mother knew that I had sent you this letter, she should never love me. No more I write to you at this time, but Holy Ghost have you in keeping. Written in haste, on Saint Peter's day, by candle light.

By your cousin,

Elizabeth Clere.

St. Peter's Day, Saturday,
    29th of June, 1454.

5

TUDOR TIMES

WILLIAM P. HAUGAARD

Elizabeth and the English Reformation, 1968

Queen Elizabeth I, 1533 - 1603

Queen Elizabeth was the real enemy of the puritans and the precisians before them. On this, all recent interpreters agree. The effective governorship of the church by a monarch is distasteful to the twentieth century, but the consequences of Elizabeth's role are much more congenial to modern tastes and values.

She introduced a lay voice into the rule of the church and, by her determined but restrained use of authority, she endowed the church with a significant degree of independence from English legislators and other government officials. Many churches since the Reformation have struggled with the problem of integrating lay authority with that of the ordained clergy. Elizabeth's solution depended heavily on the ability and commitment of the sovereign but, in her hands, the church fared well. She refused to allow the clergy to become the sole arbiters of moral, political, and religious questions as both papist and presbyterian would have had it. She insisted that an outward liturgical and clerical discipline be maintained to protect congregations from dissident clerics. She reminded the highest councils of the church that ecclesiastical decisions must take account not only of 'principle' but also of human reality measured in political and social terms. At its worst, this could mean a Christianity captive to worldliness and political expediency. At its best, it could ensure the recognition, sometimes absent in religious circles, that the so-called 'secular' orders of human life possess an integrity of their own. A church which ignores that integrity either retreats into irrelevant pious sentimentality or attempts to impose a demoniacal clerical tyranny.

The future Church of England turned out to be in the design of Queen Elizabeth rather than in that pattern which the militant reformers proposed in Convocation in 1563. If the leaders of the sixteenth century were to be arranged according to their influence on the eventual character of anglicanism, the first rank would include only two figures: the martyred cleric, Thomas Cranmer, and the royal laywoman, Elizabeth Tudor.

SIR WALTER RALEIGH, 1861 - 1922

The Age of Elizabeth, 1917

Elizabeth I to Parliament, 1559

But now that the public Care of governing the Kingdom is laid upon me, to draw upon me also the Cares of Marriage may seem a point of inconsiderate Folly. Yea, to satisfy you, I have already joined myself in Marriage to an Husband, namely, the Kingdom of England. And behold, said she, which I marvel ye have forgotten, the pledge of this my Wedlock and Marriage with my Kingdom. And therewith she drew the ring from the Finger, and shewed it, wherewith at her Coronation she had in a set form of words solemnly given herself in Marriage to her Kingdom . . .

And to me it shall be a full satisfaction, both for the memorial of my Name, and for my Glory also, if, when I shall let my last breath, it be engraven upon my Marble Tomb: Here lieth Elizabeth, which Reigned a Virgin, and died a Virgin.

WILLIAM BIRCH

Song between the Queen's Majesty and England, 1559

Here is my hand
My dear lover England,
I am thine both with mind and heart
For ever to endure,
Thou mayst be sure,
Until death we two do part.

QUEEN ELIZABETH I, 1533 - 1603

When I was fair and young and favour graced me,
Of many was I sought their mistress for to be,
But I did scorn them all and answered them therefore,
Go, go, go, seek some other where,
        Importune me no more.

How many weeping eyes I made to pine with woe,
How many sighing hearts I have no skill to show,
Yet I the prouder grew, and answered them therefore,
Go, go, go, seek some other where,
        Importune me no more.

Then spake fair Venus' son, that proud victorious boy,
And said, fine dame since that you have been so coy,
I will so pluck your plumes that you shall say no more,
Go, go, go, seek some other where,
        Importune me no more.

When he had spake these words such change grew in my
    breast,
That neither day nor night since that I could take any rest,
Then lo, I did repent of that I said before,
Go, go, go, seek some other where,
        Importune me no more.

*   *   *

ST. TERESA OF AVILA, 1515 - 1582

The Way of Perfection, c 1562
Translated by a Discalced Carmelite, 1942

St. Teresa to her nuns:
You will know, daughters, whether you are making progress, if each one of you regards herself as the most worthless of all, and shows it by her deeds, for the profit and good of others. She is not the most advanced who has great sweetness in prayer, ecstasies, visions, and other favours of the same kind, which the Lord may grant, but the value of which we have to wait until the next world to estimate rightly. The former are current coin, a revenue which does not fail, they are a perpetual inheritance, and not a quit rent, which may be redeemed. Such are the great virtues of humility, mortification, and that strict obedience which will not, on a single point, go against what the Superior commands, for you truly know that God commands it, since the Superior stands in His place. I specially recommend obedience to you, for it seems to me that without it you cannot be nuns, but I will say no more about it, as I am speaking to nuns who seem to me to be good, or at least they desire to be so; I permit myself no more than one word concerning so well-known and important a matter, that it may not be forgotten . . .

Think also of those many married women,—I know some of them,—persons in good society, who, with serious illnesses, and cruel sufferings, dare not complain, lest they should annoy their husbands. What? sinner that I am! do we come here to be treated better than they are? See how free you are from the great troubles of the world! Learn to suffer a little for the love of God, without everybody knowing about it. Here is a woman very unhappily married, but so that her husband shall not be told that she speaks of it and complains, she suffers many miseries without unburdening herself to anyone; and should we not endure, unknown to all but God and ourselves, those evils that He sends us for our sins? Especially as complaints in no way appease the trouble.

*   *   *

WILLIAM SHAKESPEARE, 1564 - 1616

The Tempest, 1611

"Sit then, and talk with her, she is thine own"

Prospero. Then, as my gift and thine own acquisition
    Worthily purchas'd, take my daughter: but
    If thou dost break her virgin knot before
    All sanctimonious ceremonies may
    With full and holy rite be minister'd,
    No sweet aspersion shall the heavens let fall
    To make this contract grow; but barren hate,
    Sour-ey'd disdain and discord shall bestrew
    The union of your bed with weeds so loathly
    That you shall hate it both: therefore take heed,
    As Hymen's lamps shall light you.

Ferdinand. As I hope
    For quiet days, fair issue and long life,
    With such love as 'tis now, the murkiest den,
    The most opportune place, the strong'st suggestion
    Our worser genius can, shall never melt
    Mine honour into lust, to take away
    The edge of that day's celebration
    When I shall think, or Phoebus' steeds are founder'd
    Or Night kept chain'd below.

Prospero. Fairly spoke:
  Sit then, and talk with her, she is thine own.

Twelfth Night, 1600

"In delay there lies no plenty"

> O mistress mine! where are you roaming?
> O! stay and hear; your true love's coming,
> That can sing both high and low.
> Trip no further, pretty sweeting;
> Journeys end in lovers meeting,
> Every wise man's son doth know.
>
> What is love? 'tis not hereafter;
> Present mirth hath present laughter;
> What's to come is still unsure:
> In delay there lies no plenty;
> Then come kiss me, sweet and twenty.
> Youth's a stuff will not endure.

"And what's her history?"
"A blank, my lord. She never told her love"

Viola. My father had a daughter lov'd a man,
> As it might be, perhaps, were I a woman,
> I should your lordship.

Duke. And what's her history?

Viola. A blank, my lord. She never told her love,
> But let concealment, like a worm i' the bud,
> Feed on her damask cheek: she pin'd in thought,
> And with a green and yellow melancholy,
> She sat like Patience on a monument,
> Smiling at grief. Was not this love indeed?

6

SEVENTEENTH AND EIGHTEENTH CENTURIES

ROBERT HERRICK, 1591 - 1674

To The Virgins, To Make Much Of Time

> Gather ye rosebuds while ye may,
> Old Time is still a-flying:
> And this same flower that smiles to-day
> To-morrow will be dying.
>
> The glorious lamp of heaven, the sun,
> The higher he's a-getting,
> The sooner will his race be run,
> And nearer he's to setting.
>
> That age is best which is the first,
> When youth and blood are warmer;
> But being spent, the worse, and worst
> Times still succeed the former.
>
> Then be not coy, but use your time,
> And while ye may, go marry:
> For having lost but once your prime,
> You may for ever tarry.

An Epitaph Upon A Virgin

> Here a solemn fast we keep,
> While all beauty lies asleep
> Hushed be all things; (no noise here)
> But the toning of a tear:
> Or a sigh of such as bring
> Cowslips for her covering.

ANDREW MARVELL, 1621 - 1678

An Epitaph

> Enough; and leave the rest to Fame!
> 'Tis to commend her, but to name.
> Courtship which, living, she declined,
> When dead, to offer were unkind:
> Nor can the truest wit, or friend,
> Without detracting, her commend.
>
> To say— she lived a virgin chaste
> In this age loose and all unlaced;
> Nor was, when vice is so allowed,
> Of virtue or ashamed or proud;
> That her soul was on Heaven so bent,
> No minute but it came and went;
> That, ready her last debt to pay,
> She summ'd her life up every day;
> Modest as morn, as mid-day bright,
> Gentle as evening, cool as night:
> —'Tis true; but all too weakly said.
> 'Twas more significant, she's dead.

*   *   *

ON GROWING OLDER
(A Mother Superior's Prayer)

Framed, in Lady Chapel, Rochester Cathedral
Believed to be 17th century

Lord, Thou knowest better than I know myself that I am growing older, and will some day be old.

Keep me from getting talkative, and particularly from the fatal habit of thinking I must say something on every subject and on every occasion.

Release me from craving to try to straighten out everybody's affairs.

Keep my mind free from the recital of endless details—give me wings to get to the point.

I ask for grace enough to listen to the tales of others' pains. Help me to endure them with patience.

But seal my lips on my own aches and pains—they are increasing, and my love of rehearsing them becomes sweeter as the years go by.

Teach me the glorious lesson that occasionally it is possible that I may be mistaken.

Keep me reasonably sweet; I do not want to be a saint—some of them are so hard to live with—but a sour old woman is one of the crowning works of the devil.

Make me thoughtful, but not moody; helpful, but not bossy. With my vast store of wisdom it seems a pity not to use it all, but Thou knowest, Lord, that I want a few friends at the end.

SIR RICHARD STEELE, 1672 - 1729

The Spinster: in Defence of the Woollen Manufactures, 1719

This Difcourfe is written in the Behalf of the Needy and Diftrefs'd, in Oppofition to the Wealthy and Powerful: who, I fear, may confpire for their own Ends, to leave the Afflictions and Complaints of their miferable Fellow-Subjects and Fellow-Creatures neglected, and unreliev'd; I fhall continue it from time to time, during the Difpute between the Dealers concern'd in the Woollen and Callico Manufactures.

But tho' my prefent Opinion is clearly on the Side of the Cloathing made from our own Wool, I fhall not be Deaf to Callico.

And if any Gentlewoman, dating her felf at the prefent Writing and Time of Year in *England,* and in Callico, fhall write her Thoughts to *Rebecca Woollpack,* Spinfter, at Mr. *Roberts's* in *Warwick-lane,* Poft paid, (for the Woollen Manufacture cannot at prefent bear Poftage) fhe fhall have a fair and candid Anfwer.

I write my felf Spinfter, because the Laws of my Country call me fo, and I think that Name, us'd in all Writings and Instruments as the Addition and Distinction of a Maiden or fingle Woman of this Ifland, denotes to us, that the general Expectation of our Lawgivers was, that the Induftry of female Manufacturers would be moft laudably employ'd this way, and therefore they gave the Office of the Spinner as a Title to the Gentlewoman.

JOSEPHINE KAMM

Hope Deferred
Girls' Education in English History, 1965

Elizabeth Elstob, 1683 - 1756

A woman with a genuine love of scholarship was Elizabeth Elstob, born in 1683 the daughter of a Newcastle merchant. Elizabeth's parents died when she was a small child, and her guardian—an uncle—stubbornly insisted that one tongue was enough for a woman and refused to let her learn Latin. Her aunt, who was less censorius, helped the girl to learn some French; and then, alone, Elizabeth studied Latin, Greek and Anglo-Saxon, which she found both easy and enjoyable. Her brother William, himself an Anglo-Saxon scholar, advised her to continue these studies; and in Oxford, where she kept house for him, she was encouraged by the foremost scholars of the day. She was twenty-six when she published her first book, an *English-Saxon Homily on the Nativity of St. Gregory.* It aroused the admiration of Oxford scholars, who often spoke of her as a female student of the University, and of her friends, who called her the Saxon Lady. Six years later—in 1715—she issued her *Rudiments of Grammar for the English Saxon Tongue;* and had started work on an ambitious book of *Saxon Homilies* when her brother died, leaving her penniless. Realizing that she could not live on the proceeds of her scholarship, Elizabeth hurriedly left Oxford and opened a little dame school at Evesham in Worcestershire, where she was paid about 4d. a week for each child. Through the influence of friends, among them Mrs. Pendarves (later Mrs. Delaney) and Mrs. Chapone, mother-in-law of the famous Mrs. Hester Chapone, who petitioned the Queen on her behalf, she could have been appointed mistress of a boarding school for the daughters of the nobility, or head of a charity school; but she refused both offers, the former because she preferred to teach the village children, the latter because she did not feel competent to teach spinning and knitting. In the end she was persuaded to accept the post of governess to the children of the Duke and Duchess of Portland, and remained in their household until her death at the age of seventy-three. If Elizabeth Elstob had done nothing to raise the standard of girls' education, she had proved in her own self-training that a woman was capable of opening fresh paths of investigation in the pursuit of learning. But she and the other seventeenth-century women who loved to study worked of their own volition, relying on their own intelligence and enthusiasm since their formal education was no more advanced than that of any of the other girls of the period.

OLIVER GOLDSMITH, 1728 - 1774

The Citizen of the World or Letters from a Chinese Philosopher residing in London to his Friends in the East, 1762

On the great number of old maids and bachelors in London. Some of the causes.

Lately in company with my friend in black, whose conversation is now both my amusement and instruction, I could not avoid observing the great numbers of old bachelors and maiden ladies with which this city seems to be over-run ...
As for old maids, continued I, they should not be treated with so much severity, because I suppose none would be so if they could. No lady in her senses would choose to make a subordinate figure at christenings and lyings-in, when she might be the principal herself; nor curry favour with a sister-in-law, when she might command an husband, nor toil in preparing custards, when she might lie abed and give directions how they ought to be made, nor stifle all her sensations in demure formality, when she might with matrimonial freedom shake her acquaintance by the hand, and wink at a double entendre. No lady could be so very silly as to live single, if she could help it. I consider an unmarried lady declining into the vale of years, as one of those charming countries bordering on China that lies waste for want of proper inhabitants. We are not to accuse the country, but the ignorance of its neighbours, who are insensible of its beauties, though at liberty to enter and cultivate the soil.
Indeed, Sir, replied my companion, you are very little acquainted with the English ladies to think they are old maids against their will. I dare venture to affirm that you can hardly select one of them all, but has had frequent offers of marriage, which either pride or avarice has not made her reject. Instead of thinking it a disgrace, they take every occasion to boast of their former cruelty; a soldier does not exult more when he counts over the wounds he has received, than a female veteran when she relates the wounds she has formerly given: exhaustless when she begins a narrative of the former death-dealing power of her eyes. She tells of the knight in gold lace, who died with a single frown, and never rose again till

37

—— he was married to his maid: Of the squire, who being cruelly denied, in a rage, flew to the window, and lifting up the sash, threw himself in an agony —— into his arm chair: Of the parson, who, crossed in love, resolutely swallowed opium, which banished the stings of despised love by —— making him sleep. In short, she talks over her former losses with pleasure, and, like some tradesmen, finds consolation in the many bankruptcies she had suffered.

For this reason, whenever I see a superannuated beauty still unmarried, I tacitly accuse her either of pride, avarice, coquetry, or affectation.

MARY WOLLSTONECRAFT, 1759 - 1797

A Vindication of the Rights of Woman, 1792

"The bitter bread of dependence"

Girls who have been thus weakly educated are often cruelly left by their parents without any provision, and, of course, are dependent on not only the reason, but the bounty of their brothers. These brothers are, to view the fairest side of the question, good sort of men, and give as a favour what children of the same parents had an equal right to. In this equivocal humiliating situation a docile female may remain some time with a tolerable degree of comfort. But when the brother marries—a probable circumstance—from being considered as the mistress of the family, she is viewed with averted looks as an intruder, an unnecessary burden on the benevolence of the master of the house and his new partner.

Who can recount the misery which many unfortunate beings, whose minds and bodies are equally weak, suffer in such situations—unable to work, and ashamed to beg? The wife, a cold-hearted, narrow-minded woman — and this is not an unfair supposition, for the present mode of education does not tend to enlarge the heart any more than the understanding — is jealous of the little kindness which her husband shows to his relations; and her sensibility not rising to humanity, she is displeased at seeing the property of *her* children lavished on an helpless sister.

These are matters of fact, which have come under my eye again and again. The consequence is obvious; the wife has recourse to cunning to undermine the habitual affection which she is afraid openly to oppose; and neither tears nor caresses are spared till the spy is worked out of her home, and thrown on the world, unprepared for its difficulties; or sent, as a great effort of generosity, or from some regard to propriety, with a small stipend, and an uncultivated mind, into joyless solitude. These two women may be much upon a par with respect to reason and humanity, and, changing situations, might have acted just the same selfish part; but had they been differently educated, the case would also have been very different. The wife would not have had that sensibility, of which self is the centre, and reason might have taught her not to expect, and not even to be flattered by, the affection of her husband, if it led him to violate prior duties. She would wish not to love him merely because he loved her, but on account of his virtues; and the sister might have been able to struggle for herself instead of eating the bitter bread of dependence.

HANNAH MORE, 1745 - 1833

Strictures on the Modern System of Female Education, 1799

Their new course of education, and the habits of life, and elegance of dress connected with it, peculiarly unfits them for the active duties of their own very important condition; while with frivolous eagerness and second-hand opportunities, they run to snatch a few of those showy acquirements which decorate the great. This is done apparently with one or other of these views; either to make their fortune by marriage, or if that fail, to qualify them to become teachers of others: hence the abundant multiplication of superficial wives, and of incompetent and illiterate governesses . . .

Since then there is a season when the youthful must cease to be young, and the beautiful to excite admiration; to grow old gracefully is perhaps one of the rarest and most valuable arts which can be taught to woman. It is for this sober season of life that education should lay up its rich resources. However disregarded they may hitherto have been, they will be wanted now. When admirers fall away, and flatterers become mute, the mind will not be driven to retire into itself, and if it find no entertainment at home, it will be driven back again upon the world with increased force. Yet forgetting this, do we not seem to educate our daughters, exclusively, for the transient period of youth, when it is to maturer life we ought to advert? Do we not educate them for a crowd, forgetting that they are to live at home? for the world, and not for themselves? for show, and not for use? for time, and not for eternity? . . .

But let us not forget, in the insolence of acknowledged superiority, that it was religion and chastity, operating on the romantic spirit of those times, which establish the despotic sway of woman; and though she now no longer looks down on her adoring votaries, from the pedestal to which an absurd idolatry had lifted her, yet let her remember that it is the same religion and chastity which once raised her to such an elevation, that must still furnish the noblest energies of her character.

M. G. JONES, 1880 - 1955

Hannah More, 1952

The five More sisters, Mary, Elizabeth, Sarah, Hannah, and Martha, were pious, intelligent, and highly competent young women. Educated by their parents, they were sent out into the world unusually well prepared to earn their living . . .
Jacob More . . . became master of a poorly endowed charity school at Stapleton, three miles outside Bristol, married Mary Grace, taught his schoolboys and his five daughters, and invited relays of unfortunate prisoners, whom the persistent French Wars deposited in the neighbourhood, to polish his

children's knowledge of the French language. His daughters, well equipped, established one of the best-known schools for girls in the eighteenth century, and retired from their labours in 1790 with a comfortable competence ...

Early in her childhood she discovered to her proud but uneasy parents an ambition for learning unusual among women. Responding to her eager request to study classics and mathematics, Jacob More taught her the rudiments of Latin and sent her during her Bristol schooldays to continue her Latin studies under James Newton, the distinguished Tutor of the Bristol Baptist Academy, thus preparing the way for Horace Walpole's encomium upon her Latin in later years. But Jacob More's instruction of his daughter in mathematics came to an abrupt end when he discovered that Hannah's ability was superior to that of the schoolboys under his care. Mathematical prowess such as hers threatened to be was unfeminine and not to be encouraged ...

The London to which Hannah More had the entree in the middle 'seventies was a little London of elderly and middle-aged men and women. Samuel Johnson was over sixty-five; Soame Jenyns was seventy; David Garrick was sixty-two when he died in 1779; Joshua Reynolds was in the early fifties, and the Blue Stocking ladies of her acquaintance, Mrs. Montagu, Mrs. Vesey, Mrs. Carter, Mrs. Chapone, were by many years the seniors of the young woman from Bristol. The eager interest and enthusiasm of an intelligent and good-looking young woman was not unwelcome to the distinguished men and women who opened their doors to her.

A life of eighty-nine years, stretching across one of the most complex and changing periods of English history, offers ample room and verge enough for the discovery of inconsistencies of conduct and faults of character. They may be found without difficulty in Hannah More's life. An old-fashioned Tory who wore the radical insignia of the abolition of the slave trade and the provision of instruction for the poor, an anti-feminist who enjoyed a freedom condemned by her as unsuitable for other women, a denouncer of plays who permitted the re-publication of her own dramatic writings does not appear as a model of consistency. Nor does her life disguise her faults of character. 'She was', said wise old Marianne Thornton, who knew her well, 'a little hardened by contumely and criticism, a little spoilt by her success.' She was too great a respecter of persons, a fault she recognized and deplored, and she did not lack the spiritual vanity which has been called 'the besetting sin of Evangelicals'. All this must be admitted, but the allegations of religious hypocrisy and worldly-mindedness made by William Shaw and Thomas de Quincey and other minor detractors cannot stand against the evidence of her life or the bulk of contemporary opinion. Her singleness of aim and generosity of temper are everywhere apparent. She emerges as a woman of integrity, piety, and moral courage, on whose tongue was the law of kindness. 'Don't believe anything you hear that she said or did,' wrote Miss Thornton, the last of Lord Macaulay's generation, to one of the younger generation thirty years after Hannah More's death, 'she was a fine creature overflowing with affection and feeling and generosity.'

7

THE ENGLISH GOVERNESS

SARAH TOMLINSON, 1859

'. . . it seemed as if there were no way in which an unmarried lady could earn a living but by taking a situation as governess, for which post she was often unfit by nature and education, or want of education.'

*   *   *

ELLEN WEETON, 1776 - 1844

Journal of a Governess, 1807 - 1811
Edited Edward Hall, 1936

To Mrs. Whitehead: *May 23, 1809*
A little while ago I had a very wild scheme in agitation, which was, to traverse Wales on foot; a mode of travelling I should prefer, were I ever so wealthy — but when I reflect on the many insults a female is liable to, if alone, I find it impracticable. My ignorance of the language too, is another obstacle. My plan was, to get acquainted with some decent Welsh farmer's family and by their means to get acquainted with another; and so on, as long as the chain would last; and board with each family as long as I staid, and to dress in the plainest garments I had, that I might attract less notice. I must not think of putting such a scheme in practise. If I was but a man, now! I could soon do it.

. . . and as to the old-maid, I may perhaps lose that title entirely before twelve months are over; not that I so much regard the man, but - to avoid the finger of contempt, the smile of ridicule. If it were not for that, I am too happy as I am to wish for any change. An old maid is a stock for everyone to laugh at. Every article of dress, every word, every movement is satirized. Boys play tricks upon them, and are applauded. Girls sneer at them, and are unreproved. - Upon my word, I think I will write an essay upon the pitiable state of old maids for some Magazine or Paper.

> But I must make haste and do it,
> Whilst I can put,
> > Your sincerely
> > > Affectionate sister,
> > > > E.W. to it.

To Miss Winkley *Dove's-Nest. Nov. 21. 1810.*

I can write but a short letter, for just now I am altogether agitation and fret; that same agreeable Mr.———— I once mentioned before, from Lancaster, is here again. I wish he were either less agreeable, or would take himself away; his presence is too much for me, I shall be downright ill if he stays much longer. I do most sincerely wish him gone.

I am too humble, too insignificant, too ignorant, and too poor to excite any attention from him. Such a man should not go loose; he should either marry, or be confined, for he is calculated to win characters ten times more exalted than I am, and almost ten thousand of them. He is so like my brother in mind, but superior to him in disposition and figure - These sentiments ought to have been kept within my bosom. I *earnestly* beg of you to keep the secret *better than I have done* . . .

P.S. Burn this letter, my dear friend, as soon as possible; let *no one* see it.

(Mr. S. left on the 24th).

To Mrs. Whitehead:

"If we were together," say you, "we could plan; or if you would write, I could present it with confidence." If I did write, I must be merely your amanuensis; for my own genius has been so strongly repressed, has so long lain dormant, that now I fear it could produce nothing. There was a time, when I think (may I say it without vanity?) something might have been done; I feel confident I could have risen to something higher, something greater, but such pains were taken by my mother to repress my too great ardour for literature, that any talents I then possessed as a child, have been nearly extinguished, and it is too late now to blow them into flame. When I read the Biography of celebrated characters, my heart will yet burn within me, and I could exclaim, "Oh, why have I been so chained down in obscurity? Why have I been so secluded from every species of mental improvement? Living entirely amongst the illiterate, and unable to procure books, a dark cloud has invariably hung over me - I know little more than this - that I am very ignorant."

*   *   *

CHARLOTTE BRONTË, 1816 - 1855

Letter written whilst herself a governess
Edited M. Spark, 1954

Charlotte Brontë to Emily J. Brontë

Stonegappe,
June 8th, 1839

Dearest Lavinia,

. . . I have striven hard to be pleased with my new situation. The country, the house, and the grounds are, as I have said, divine. But, alack-a-day! there is such a thing as seeing all beautiful around you - pleasant woods, winding white paths, green lawns, and blue sunshiny sky - and not having a free moment or a free thought left to enjoy them in. The children are constantly with me, and more riotous, perverse, unmanageable cubs never grew. As for correcting them, I soon

45

quickly found that was entirely out of the question: they are to do as they like. A complaint to Mrs. Sidgwick brings only black looks upon oneself, and unjust, partial excuses to screen the children. I have tried that plan once. It succeeded so notably that I shall try it no more. I said in my last letter that Mrs. Sidgwick did not know me. I now begin to find that she does not intend to know me, that she cares nothing in the world about me except to contrive how the greatest possible quantity of labour may be squeezed out of me, and to that end she overwhelms me with oceans of needlework, yards of cambric to hem, muslin nightcaps to make, and, above all things, dolls to dress. I do not think she likes me at all, because I can't help being shy in such an entirely novel scene, surrounded as I have hitherto been by strange and constantly changing faces. I see now more clearly than I have ever done before that a private governess has no existence, is not considered as a living and rational being except as connected with the wearisome duties she has to fulfil. Whilst she is teaching the children, working for them, amusing them, it is all right. If she steals a moment for herself she is a nuisance. Nevertheless, Mrs. Sidgwick is univerally considered an amiable woman. Her manners are fussily affable. She talks a great deal, but as it seems to me not much to the purpose. Perhaps I may like her better after a while. At present I have no call to her. Mr. Sidgwick is in my opinion a hundred times better - less profession, less bustling condescension, but a far kinder heart. It is very seldom that he speaks to me, but when he does I always feel happier and more settled for some minutes after. He never asks me to wipe the children's smutty noses or tie their shoes or fetch their pinafores or set them a chair. One of the pleasantest afternoons I have spent here - indeed, the only one at all pleasant - was when Mr. Sidgwick walked out with his children, and I had orders to follow a little behind. As he strolled on through his fields with his magnificent Newfoundland dog at his side, he looked very like what a frank, wealthy, Conservative gentleman ought to be. He spoke freely and unaffectedly to the people he met, and though he indulged his children and allowed them to tease himself far too much, he would not suffer them grossly to insult others.

I am getting quite to have a regard for the Carter family. At home I should not care for them, but here they are friends.

Mr. Carter was at Mirfield yesterday and saw Anne. He says she was looking uncommonly well. Poor girl, *she* must indeed wish to be at home. As to Mrs. Collins' report that Mrs. Sidgwick intended to keep me permanently, I do not think that such was ever her design. Moreover, I would not stay without some alterations. For instance, this burden of sewing would have to be removed. It is too bad for anything. I never in my whole life had my time so fully taken up. Next week we are going to Swarcliffe, Mr. Greenwood's place near Harrogate, to stay three weeks or a month. After that time I hope Miss Hoby will return. Don't show this letter to papa or aunt, only to Branwell. They will think I am never satisfied, wherever I am. I complain to you because it is a relief, and really I have had some unexpected mortifications to put up with. However, things may mend, but Mrs. Sidgwick expects me to do things that I cannot do - to love her children and be entirely devoted to them. I am really very well. I am so sleepy that I can write no more. I must leave off. Love to all. - Good-bye.
Direct your next despatch - J. Greenwood, Esq., Swarcliffe, near Harrogate.

C. Brontë

Charlotte Brontë to Miss Wooler, her old schoolmistress, January 30th, 1846
I always feel a peculiar satisfaction when I hear of your enjoying yourself, because it proves that there really is such a thing as retributive justice even in this world. You worked hard; you denied yourself all pleasure, almost all relaxation, in your youth, and in the prime of life; now you are free, and that while you have still, I hope, many years of vigour and health in which you can enjoy freedom. Besides, I have another and very egotistical motive for being pleased: it seems that even 'a lone woman' can be happy, as well as cherished wives and proud mothers. I am glad of that. I speculate much on the existence of unmarried and never-to-be-married women now-a-days; and I have already got to the point of considering that there is no more respectable character on this earth than an unmarried woman, who makes her own way through life quietly, perseveringly, without support of husband or brother;

and who, having attained the age of forty-five or upwards, retains in her possession a well-regulated mind, a disposition to enjoy simple pleasures, and fortitude to support inevitable pains, sympathy with the sufferings of others, and willingness to relieve want as far as her means extend.

Shirley, 1849

Mrs. Pryor - on her days as a governess, before marriage
"You told me before you wished to be a governess; but, my dear, if you remember, I did not encourage the idea. I have been a governess myself great part of my life . . .
It was my lot to enter a family of considerable pretensions to good birth and mental superiority, and the members of which also believed that 'on them was perceptible' an usual endowment of the 'Christian graces'; that all their hearts were regenerate, and their spirits in a peculiar state of discipline. I was early given to understand that 'as I was not their equal,' so I could not expect 'to have their sympathy.' It was in no sort concealed from me that I was held a 'burden and a restraint in society.' The gentlemen, I found, regarded me as a 'tabooed woman,' to whom 'they were interdicted from granting the usual privileges of the sex,' and yet who 'annoyed them by frequently crossing their path.' The ladies too made it plain that they thought me 'a bore.' The servants, it was signified, 'detested me'; *why*, I could never clearly comprehend. My pupils, I was told, 'however much they might love me, and how deep soever the interest I might take in them, could not be my friends.' It was intimated that I must 'live alone, and never transgress the invisible but rigid line which established the difference between me and my employers.' My life in this house was sedentary, solitary, constrained, joyless, toilsome. The dreadful crushing of the animal spirits, the ever-prevailing sense of friendlessness and homelessness consequent on this state of things, began ere long to produce mortal effects on my constitution - I sickened. The lady of the house told me coolly I was the victim of 'wounded vanity.' She hinted, that if I did not make an effort to quell my 'ungodly discontent,' to cease 'murmuring against God's appointment,' and to cultivate the profound humility befitting my station, my mind would very likely 'go to pieces' on the rock that wrecked most

of my sisterhood - morbid self-esteem; and that I should die an inmate of a lunatic asylum.

"I said nothing to Mrs. Hardman; it would have been useless: but to her eldest daughter I one day dropped a few observations, which were answered thus: - There were hardships, she allowed, in the position of a governess: 'doubtless they had their trials: but,' she averred, with a manner it makes me smile now to recall - 'but it must be so. *She* (Miss H.) had neither view, hope, nor *wish* to see these things remedied: for, in the inherent constitution of English habits, feelings, and prejudices, there was no possibility that they should be. Governesses,' she observed, 'must ever be kept in a sort of isolation: it is the only means of maintaining that distance which the reserve of English manners and the decorum of English families exact.'

"I remember I sighed as Miss Hardman quitted my bedside: she caught the sound, and turning, said severely - 'I fear, Miss Grey, you have inherited in fullest measure the worst sin of our fallen nature - the sin of pride. You are proud, and therefore you are ungrateful too. Mamma pays you a handsome salary; and, if you had average sense, you would thankfully put up with much that is fatiguing to do and irksome to bear, since it is so well made worth your while'. . .

"I remember," continued Mrs. Pryor, after a pause, "another of Miss H.'s observations, which she would utter with quite a grand air. '*We,*' she would say, - '*We* need the imprudences, extravagances, mistakes, and crimes of a certain number of fathers to sow the seed from which *we* reap the harvest of governesses. The daughters of tradespeople, however well-educated, must necessarily be underbred, and as such unfit to be inmates of *our* dwellings, or guardians of *our* children's minds and persons. *We* shall ever prefer to place those about *our* offspring, who have been born and bred with somewhat of the same refinement as *ourselves.*' ". . .

"All I mean to say, my dear, is, that you had better not attempt to be a governess, as the duties of the position would be too severe for your constitution. Not one word of disrespect would I breathe towards either Mrs. or Miss Hardman; only, recalling my own experience, I cannot but feel that, were you to fall under auspices such as theirs, you would contend a while courageously with your doom: then you would pine and grow too weak for your work; you would come home - if you had a home - broken down. Those languishing years would follow, of which none but the invalid and her immediate friends feel the heart-sickness and know the burden: consumption or decline would close the chapter. Such is the history of many a life: I would not have it yours."

*　　*　　*

CHARLES DICKENS, 1812 - 1870

Martin Chuzzlewit, 1843

Miss Pinch is rescued by her brother, Tom
"I am sorry to inform you that we are not at all satisfied with your sister."
"We are very much *dis*satisfied with her," observed the lady.
"I'd never say another lesson to Miss Pinch if I was to be beat to death for it!" sobbed the pupil.
"Sophia!" cried her father. "Hold your tongue!"
"Will you allow me to inquire what your ground of dis-satisfaction is?" asked Tom.
"Yes," said the gentleman, "I will. I don't recognise it as a right; but I will. Your sister has not the slightest innate power of commanding respect. It has been a constant source of difference between us. Although she has been in this family for some time, and although the young lady who is now present has almost, as it were, grown up under her tuition, that young lady has no respect for her. Miss Pinch has been perfectly unable to command my daughter's respect, or to win my daughter's confidence. Now," said the gentleman, allowing the palm of his hand to fall gravely down upon the table: "I maintain that there is something radically wrong in that! You, as her brother, may be disposed to deny it—"
"I beg your pardon sir," said Tom. "I am not at all disposed to deny it. I am sure that there is something radically wrong: radically monstrous: in that."
"Good Heavens!" cried the gentleman, looking round the room with dignity, "what do I find to be the case! what results obtrude themselves upon me as flowing from this weakness of character on the part of Miss Pinch! What are my feelings as a father, when, after my desire (repeatedly expressed to Miss

50

Pinch, as I think she will not venture to deny) that my daughter should be choice in her expressions, genteel in her deportment, as becomes her station in life, and politely distant to her inferiors in society, I find her, only this very morning, addressing Miss Pinch herself as a beggar!"

"A beggarly thing," observed the lady, in correction.

"Which is worse," said the gentleman, triumphantly; "which is worse. A beggarly thing. A low, coarse, despicable expression!"

"Most despicable," cried Tom. "I am glad to find that there is a just appreciation of it here."

"So just, sir," said the gentleman, lowering his voice to be the more impressive. "So just, that, but for my knowing Miss Pinch to be an unprotected young person, an orphan, and without friends, I would, as I assured Miss Pinch, upon my veracity and personal character, a few minutes ago, I would have severed the connexion between us at that moment and from that time."

"Bless my soul, sir!" cried Tom, rising from his seat; for he was now unable to contain himself any longer; "don't allow such considerations as those to influence you, pray. They don't exist, sir. She is not unprotected. She is ready to depart this instant. Ruth, my dear, get your bonnet on!"

"Oh, a pretty family!" cried the lady. "Oh, he's her brother! There's no doubt about that!"

"As little doubt, madam," said Tom, "as that the young lady yonder is the child of your teaching, and not my sister's. Ruth, my dear, get your bonnet on!"

"When you say, young man," interposed the brass-and-copper founder, haughtily, "with that impertinence which is natural to you, and which I therefore do not condescend to notice further, that the young lady, my eldest daughter, has been educated by any one but Miss Pinch, you - I needn't proceed. You comprehend me fully. I have no doubt you are used to it."

"Sir!" cried Tom, after regarding him in silence for some little time. "If you do not understand what I mean, I will tell you. If you do understand what I mean, I beg you not to repeat that mode of expressing yourself in answer to it. My meaning is, that no man can expect his children to respect what he degrades."

"Ha, ha, ha!" laughed the gentleman. "C..nt! cant! The common cant!"

51

"The common story, sir!" said Tom; "the story of a common mind. Your governess cannot win the confidence and respect of your children, forsooth! Let her begin by winning yours, and see what happens then."

"Miss Pinch is getting her bonnet on, I trust, my dear?" said the gentleman.

"I trust she is," said Tom, forestalling the reply. "I have no doubt she is. In the meantime I address myself to you, sir. You made your statement to me, sir; you required to see me for that purpose; and I have a right to answer it. I am not loud or turbulent," said Tom, which was quite true, "though I can scarcely say as much for you, in your manner of addressing yourself to me. And I wish, on my sister's behalf, to state the simple truth."

"You may state anything you like, young man," returned the gentleman, affecting to yawn. "My dear, Miss Pinch's money."

"When you tell me," resumed Tom, who was not the less indignant for keeping himself quiet, "that my sister has no innate power of commanding the respect of your children, I must tell you it is not so; and that she has. She is as well bred, as well taught, as well qualified by nature to command respect, as any hirer of a governess you know. But when you place her at a disadvantage in reference to every servant in your house, how can you suppose, if you have the gift of common sense, that she is not in a tenfold worse position in reference to your daughters?"

"Pretty well! Upon my word," exclaimed the gentleman, "this is pretty well!"

"It is very ill, sir," said Tom. "It is very bad and mean, and wrong and cruel. Respect! I believe young people are quick enough to observe and imitate; and why or how should they respect whom no one else respects, and everybody slights? And very partial they must grow - oh, very partial! - to their studies, when they see to what a pass proficiency in those same tasks has brought their governess! Respect! Put anything the most deserving of respect before your daughters in the light in which you place her, and you will bring it down as low, no matter what it is!"

"You speak with extreme impertinence, young man," observed the gentleman.

"I speak without passion, but with extreme indignation and

contempt for such a course of treatment, and for all who practise it," said Tom. "Why, how can you, as an honest gentleman, profess displeasure or surprise at your daughter telling my sister she is something beggarly and humble, when you are for ever telling her the same thing yourself in fifty plain, out-speaking ways, though not in words; and when your very porter and footman make the same delicate announcement to all comers? As to your suspicion and distrust of her: even of her word: if she is not above their reach, you have no right to employ her."

"No right!" cried the brass-and-copper founder.

"Distinctly not," Tom answered. "If you imagine that the payment of an annual sum of money gives it to you, you immensely exaggerate its power and value. Your money is the least part of your bargain in such a case. You may be punctual in that to half a second on the clock, and yet be Bankrupt. I have nothing more to say," said Tom, much flushed and flustered, now that it was over, "except to crave permission to stand in your garden until my sister is ready."

Not waiting to obtain it, Tom walked out.

Before he had well begun to cool, his sister joined him. She was crying; and Tom could not bear that any one about the house should see her doing that.

"They will think you are sorry to go," said Tom. "You are not sorry to go?"

"No, Tom, no. I have been anxious to go for a very long time."

"Very well, then! Don't cry!" said Tom.

"I am so sorry for *you*, dear," sobbed Tom's sister.

"But you ought to be glad on my account," said Tom. "I shall be twice as happy with you for a companion. Hold up your head. There! Now we go out as we ought. Not blustering, you know, but firm and confident in ourselves."

The idea of Tom and his sister blustering, under any circumstances, was a splendid absurdity. But Tom was very far from feeling it to be so, in his excitement; and passed out at the gate with such severe determination written in his face that the porter hardly knew him again.

* * *

BARBARA STEPHEN, 1872 - 1945

Emily Davies and Girton College, 1927

"Source of better things:"
The Governesses' Benevolent Institution, 1843
Queen's College, Harley Street, 1848

About half-way through the century, economic pressure and the fashion for philanthropy brought into existence an institution which was to be the source of better things. The Governesses' Benevolent Institution, founded in 1843, came to the help of distressed governesses with loans, annuities, and asylums for the aged; but it was soon found that these measures of alleviation were quite inadequate. On the initiative of the Rev. David Laing and Miss Murray (one of Queen Victoria's maids of honour), steps were taken to establish a college for Governesses where women could qualify themselves for the profession of teaching, and pass examinations which would help them to command more reasonable salaries. In this way was founded in 1848 Queen's College, Harley Street, which produced those great pioneers of the reformation in girls' schools, Miss Beale and Miss Buss.

8

THE EDUCATIONISTS

THE SCHOOLS INQUIRY COMMISSION'S REPORT,
1868

*"We have had much evidence showing the general in-
difference of parents to girls' education, both in itself and as
compared to that of boys. It leads to a less immediate and
tangible pecuniary result; there is a long-established and
inveterate prejudice . . . that girls are less capable of mental
cultivation, and less in need of it than boys; that accomplish-
ments and what is showy and superficially attractive are what
is really essential for them; and in particular that, as regards
their relations to the other sex and the probabilities of
marriage, more solid attainments are actually disadvan-
tageous . . . It must be fully admitted that such ideas have a
very strong root in human nature . . ."*

*"It is certainly a singular fact, and one not by any means
admitting of an easy explanation," the commissioners said,
"that with these few exceptions no part of the large funds
arising from endowments for the education of the middle
classes is now, or has been for a long time past, devoted to so
important a purpose as the education of girls and young
women . . . The appropriation of almost all the educational
endowments of the country to the education of boys is felt by a
large and increasing number both of men and women to be a
cruel injustice."*

*   *   *

JOSEPHINE KAMM

How Different from Us.
A Biography of Miss Buss and Miss Beale, 1958

> *Miss Buss and Miss Beale*
> *Cupid's darts do not feel.*
> *How different from us,*
> *Miss Beale and Miss Buss.*

Owing, no doubt, to the influence of the immortal rhyme and the variations of it which have appeared, few people realise that neither Frances Mary Buss nor Dorothea Beale was immune from Cupid's darts. They were attractive young women, Dorothea, with her grave beauty, especially so. Frances Mary, with her father's pleasure in colour and texture, made up in style and elegance what she lacked in beauty. Her strong features, so like her mother's, were fore-shortened and diminished by an almost non-existent chin set on a thick throat; but one of her original pupils remembered for the rest of her life her first impression of an "elegant dark young lady, with curls and a low-necked dress", whose vigorous intensity "seemed to sweep me up like a strong wind".

According to her friend and biographer Annie E. Ridley, Frances Mary rejected more than one offer of marriage. Many Victorian daughters gave up the idea of marriage in order to act as unpaid companion to their parents: Frances Mary relinquished it in order to support hers. Whether or not this was the sole reason we do not know: but many years later she wrote: "I have had real heart-ache, such as at intervals in earlier life I had to bear: when I put aside marriage; when Mr. Laing died; and again when my dearest mother, the brave loving, strong, tender woman, left all her children. I quite believe in heart-ache! God's ways are not our ways!" . . .

There were to be many occasions when Frances Mary, feeling frail and oppressed, longed for the support and comfort of a strong right arm; and yet since it is well known that women of so powerfully dominant a type almost invariably choose a weak, dependent husband, it is more than likely that she would have chosen - as her own mother chose - a man who

56

would be child more than husband. Her chief instincts were maternal; and like many another good schoolmistress she sublimated them in the career which attracted her irresistibly. Dorothea Beale, with the same instincts, sublimated them with equal success. She, too, rejected several proposals of marriage, although she went a step further than Frances Mary, for at one period before she went to Casterton she was actually engaged. For some reason the engagement was broken. "Suffice it to say", writes her biographer Elizabeth Raikes, a past mistress of aggravating innuendo, "that Dorothea Beale knew what it was to be admired, loved, even for a short time engaged to be married. She knew also, among other experiences, what it was to sacrifice a girlish romance because it was right to put away vain regret; to forget the things that are behind, and in this matter as in others, to use any sense of personal loss in such a way that it strengthened her character."

Miss Buss' school *

The school, which had been opened without class distinctions, remained without them; and money-snobbery, the bane of many impecunious schoolgirls, did not exist, either then or at any time later. "No one asked where you lived," wrote one pupil, "how much pocket-money you had, or what your father was - he might be a bishop or a rat-catcher." And it was a point of honour among the girls to make their dresses last as long as possible.

What Frances Mary Buss had achieved in this direction few others had cared to attempt. Fourteen years after the opening of her school - as the Schools' Inquiry Commission Report showed - educational authorities were still doubtful of the wisdom of founding girls' schools which were socially "mixed".

"On . . . the question . . . of the mixture of different classes of society in the same schools, there seems much more agreement, in the direction unfavourable to such mixture, as to girls' schools than as to boys', both from general reasons

---

* The North London Collegiate School for Ladies, opened April 4, 1850; became public day school 1871 when renamed The North London Collegiate School for Girls.

and observation, and with regard to the feelings of the parents."

The movement towards a classless society which Frances Mary had begun was, of course, to spread and root itself in the educational life of the country. And just as she permitted no social distinctions, she permitted no religious distinctions either. She was - as Dorothea Beale wrote after her death - "deeply, unostentatiously religious"; and she was also infinitely tolerant. Her school, she wrote in 1868, had always been conducted "on what is here called the 'conscience clause'; that is, the parents have the right of omitting the Church of English Catechism or any part of the religious teaching they object to. Even Jewesses have received the whole of their education in the school."

This religious tolerance at a time when Jews and Catholics still suffered certain disabilities was brave and far-sighted.

BARBARA STEPHEN, 1872—1945

Emily Davies and Girton College, 1927

Letter from Miss Davies to Miss Manning, 1865
"I received my cheque for £10 from the Vice-Chancellor yesterday, for superintending the examination of girls. Miss Buss says I ought not to spend it, but to have it framed and glazed. I suppose it is the first payment ever made by the University*to a woman for a service not menial."

'A University for Maidens'
So long ago as 1847, Tennyson had portrayed in *The Princess* a college where women could enjoy the highest kind of education. The vision, though fantastic, was not forgotten; and it remained in the clouds indeed, but occasionally seen and remembered. A college for women became a definite object of aspiration to Madame Bodichon when, a couple of years later, she visited her brother Benjamin, then an undergraduate at Jesus College Cambridge. But it was too

---

* of Cambridge

soon; she was only twenty-two; and public opinion was as yet comfortably unconscious of any deficiency in the education of women. Ten years later, the deficiencies were beginning to make themselves felt. "When shall we see anything like 'a University for maidens'?" asked a writer on *Colleges for Girls* in the *Englishwoman's Journal* of February, 1859, quoting *The Princess*. The idea was becoming familiar, but Tennyson had given it to associations which were sublime, sentimental, absurd—anything rather than practical. Miss Davies set herself to bring the castle in the air down to earth, a task for whose practical difficulties her previous experience had been the best of preparations.

The meeting of schoolmistresses at Manchester on October 6, 1866, at which the subject of colleges was discussed, put the final touch to the train of events which, as Miss Davies notes in her *Family Chronicle,* "led—or drove—me to the conclusion that our case could only be met by starting a new College for Women." As she drove back from the meeting to the house at which she was staying (Mr. and Mrs. Herbert Phillip's) it was borne in upon her that there was nothing else for it. Fired with the idea, she confided it to her friends, and was soon glowing with enthusiasm and full of plans for its accomplishment. Madame Bodichon was, of course, quickly secured as an ally. . .

Before the year ended, Miss Davies had drafted a "programme," as she called it,—a short leaflet stating the need for a college which should provide for young women something analogous to what the Universities provided for young men.

Girton's first student

The first student who entered, Miss Gibson, was a former pupil of Miss Pipe, headmistress of Laleham School, Clapham Park. . .

It was though an article by Mr. Llewelyn Davies in *Macmillan's Magazine* that Miss Gibson discovered the College. She was at once inspired with the wish to enter it. What followed is best described in her own words:

"I was eighteen then, and was longing for an opportunity for study, so the information when it came in my way was deeply interesting. My school days had been cut short by money troubles at home before I was sixteen. . . . I had been for

59

three years at a private school at Clapham, a Methodist school kept by a very remarkable woman. . . . Miss Pipe was the daughter of a Manchester shopkeeper and began teaching at seventeen. When I knew her at thirty-five she was a person of ripe wisdom and intelligence, a most ingenious and inspiring teacher. One of her plans was to keep us in touch with the growth of her mind, and I remember that she read us passages from Emily Davies' *Higher Education of Women* when it was published, and when I wrote and told her of my wish to go to the new College, she was kindly and sympathetic. "As a result of the *Macmillan* article I called on Miss Davies to ask for further information. I told her that my education was very defective and asked her advice as to whether I should attempt the first entrance examination and how soon it was likely to be held. She told me that the examination might probably take place in the following June, and urged me to put my name down for it, saying it would do me no harm to fail, and that it was very important that there should be plenty of applicants. She advised me to spend the intervening months in studying Latin (of which I knew nothing) and mathematics. This advice was not easy to act on, for money was scarce . . . but I was determined to let nothing interfere with the examination, though I felt quite unprepared for it. "When it came I thoroughly enjoyed it and was immensely interested in seeing the other students, about seventeen I think in number. . .
"After the examination Miss Davies had a reception or afternoon party for the purpose of introducing the students to the Committee. It was then that I first saw Madame Bodichon, and the little talk I had with her made an outstanding event in my life. Her frank, direct manner went straight to my heart. I felt that the College meant a great deal to her, and that it was a great privilege to have a chance of helping to make it a success. . . ."

The Entrance Examination was held at the University of London (Burlington Gardens) under Miss Davies' super-intendence, and she took the opportunity of writing to Madame Bodichon while she was sitting in the room with the candidates doing their papers. She was able to tell her that it had at last been definitely decided to take Benslow House, Hitchin, for the College.

Girton's first year—Miss Davies looks back

Miss Davies to Miss Anna Richardson   June 23 (1870).
"The old students—they begin to grow venerable—separated
in a pleasant state of mind; I had a talk with them the evening
I left on the results of one year, putting it in the form of the
question whether it would be worth while to come for a year
only. The thing Miss Lloyd feels to have gained is some
appreciation of the scholarly, as distinguished from the
man-of-business way of looking at things. Miss Lumsden said
that before she came, she used to feel fearfully solitary. She
was always having said to her, 'Oh, but you're so exceptional.'
Now, she feels herself belonging to a body, and has lost the
sense of loneliness. Miss Townshend has learnt that she does
not know how to study. Before she came, she thought she did.
Also, she feels it a relief to have taken a step, from which she
could not go back even if she wished. She has got rid of the
harass of the daily self-questioning about what she had better
do with herself. Miss Gibson replied briefly that one year was
better than nothing. Miss Cook said she would rather not
come at all than that, and being asked why, explained that she
would be so sorry to go away. Miss Gibson said she should feel
that just as much at the end of the three years, to which there
was a chorus of assent."

and

PUNCH, 14th January, 1871

The Chignon At Cambridge.

At the examination lately held at Cambridge, a number of
students from the Ladies College at Hitchin passed their
"Little-go;" the first time that such undergraduates ever
underwent that ordeal. It is gratifying to be enabled to add,
that out of all those flowers of loveliness, not one was plucked.
Bachelors of Arts are likely to be made look to their laurels by
these Spinsters, and Masters must work hard or they will be
eclipsed by Mistresses, more completely than the Sun was the

other day by the Moon. And we may expect that when such competitors of both sexes come to perform upon the classical and mathematical Tripos, a Pythoness will be first upon the former, and another young lady will dance off triumphantly Senior Wrangler.

*   *   *

BLANCHE ATHENA CLOUGH, 1861 - 1960

Memoir of Anne Jemima Clough, 1820 - 1892, published 1897. First Principal of Newnham College, Cambridge, 1871 - 1892

Miss A.J. Clough's diary when twenty, 1840

Liverpool
On Friday afternoon went a-walking with Arthur* on the shore as far as Seaforth. Feel very reserved, and cannot talk till towards the end. We talked about women forming opinions, that it is not altogether necessary for everyone to know the reason why he acts thus and thus. It is possible to have the opinion without knowing it or being able to exactly express it.
Arthur leaves us in the morning . . .

October
The school and the children fill my heart and time as much as ever, but I have not begun to visit them regularly.
A good deal of proud thought, thinking too highly and too much of myself, my appearance, etc., then while at German my thoughts were distracted a good deal . . . full of love and such things. There would surely be great enjoyment in being in love. These things will rise up. Nonsense!
Many distracting thoughts about the Howards, M.'s wedding, marrying in general. My heart felt quite soft. That it would be

---

* her brother.

62

pleasant to be in love and marrying, and all that sort of thing, came into my head and unsteadied me . . .

I did indeed feel to-day a bounding happiness, as if I could run and cry out almost from joy. But I ought to work very much harder, and if I dare say so, I will.

Have had a great many idle, foolish thoughts about marriage. I cannot always keep myself steady about that. Foolish show-off thoughts will come up and bother me . . . My mind wants a good steady hard working, it is getting flimsy. That would drive out all this nonsense.

November

Just come home from walking in Bold Street. Have been giving way to all sorts of nonsense, proud and swaggering thoughts, thinking everybody was remarking me. How grand it would be if I could have a season at the Wellington Room balls! I would carry myself very high . . . in short, cut a regular flash . . . But I know better too. This won't do; all these wild fancies must be quelled, and so they shall, or I am ruined.

Recollections by Mrs. Alfred Marshall—an early student

"The first time I saw Miss Clough was at the Higher Local Examination of 1871, when her white hair and dark eyes and kindly ways made a deep impression on me. Her appearance and manners converted my father to the plan of my going to Cambridge, to which, before he saw her, he had been averse.

"In October 1871, Mary Kennedy, Ella Bulley, Edith Creak, Annie Migault, and I came to be with her at 74 Regent Street, and in the following term we were joined by Felicia Larner, and one or two others. We lived very much the life of a family : we studied together, we had our meals at one table, and in the evening we usually sat with Miss Clough in her sitting-room. We did our best to keep down household expenses : our food was very simple ; we all, including Miss Clough, not only made our beds and dusted our rooms, but we helped to wash up after meals, and we did the domestic sewing in the evening.

"During the first year at Regent Street there were certain discomforts to be put up with. We went twice a week to the

63

town gymnasium, but otherwise walks were our only form of exercise. We watched the undergraduates playing games on Parker's Piece, and envied them, and no doubt we made up for want of outdoor exercise by being rather noisy in the house, especially at meals. I believe we were all hard-working and well-intentioned, but during that first year there was a good deal of friction between Miss Clough and some of us. I think we were almost entirely to blame, and I never cease to be astonished at our want of appreciation in those days. We did not really understand her at all. I believe if she had had more weaknesses and limitations, we should have liked her better. We failed to see the great outlines of her character, her selflessness, her strong purpose, her extraordinary sympathy. She had some obvious faults of manner, and these we did see and probably exaggerated. She did not dress well, and she had a certain timidity and irresoluteness.

"The venture of women's education in Cambridge was a new one : she was, I think, a little afraid of us, and did not know what we might do next. She had not had much to do with girls of our age before, and perhaps she treated us too much like schoolgirls. She did not quite enter into our notions of fun ; perhaps she took things a little too seriously, and so she did not gain our full confidence in those early days.

"And, then, we lived too much together. I believe we should have appreciated her more if we had not been obliged to be so constantly with her. One has to see persons from a distance as well as near to appreciate them. When we moved to Merton Hall in October 1872, everything went better. . . . We had several tables for meals ; she had her own room ; when we were together it was from choice, not from necessity. We got into the habit of studying in our own rooms. We had a delightful garden, and games and more amusements, and we began to understand her better and the privilege of living with her. But it was not till I ceased to be a student that I realised her wonderful goodness and greatness."

Miss A. J. Clough recalls Newnham's first two years
"These two years were wonderfully bright and exciting, full of movement and change. There were a great variety of students with Merton and the other house in Trumpington Street. The St. John's Fellows named it Sandford, so we were Sandford

and Merton, Miss Hutchins and I. Then there were the students who lived in lodgings to be attended to, among them Miss Ogle, who was very interesting and very industrious. She was looked after by Miss Hutchins, I looked after Miss Emily Nunn. She formed a great friendship with Mrs. Smith (the widow of William Smith, who came to spend some time in Cambridge), and this was a great pleasure to her.

"There were many complications. The young people were feeling their freedom, and they wanted a little more. They agreed fairly; but still there were feuds in a mild way sometimes. And for the managers there were constant difficulties. It was as if one was picking one's way with all this large party. There was a faint path, but as we walked, I felt that the path had closed up behind us, the leader could not go back, what was done was accomplished. So one had to be very wary, very careful. They were anxious years, but one did not feel them very much, for so many kind friends were around. There was so much sympathy, so much help, and the young people were willing for the most part to be led. Their great interest in their studies, their anxieties about the examinations, the feeling that so much was being done for them, their reverence and respect for their teachers, all united to keep them steady."

ANNIE M.A.H. ROGERS 1856 - 1937

Degrees by Degrees, 1938
The Story of the Admission of Oxford Women Students to Membership of the University

The academic father of women's education in Oxford was the Delegacy of Local Examinations, created in 1857. In 1867 it applied to the Hebdomadal Council, citing the precedent of Cambridge, to examine girls, and examined the first in 1870. The experiment was not unsuccessful. In 1871 I was myself placed in the First Class of the junior candidates, and in 1873 I was fortunate enough to head the list of senior candidates. This created some little stir. Balliol and Worcester had offered exhibitions on the results of the Senior Locals, and there was nothing in the printed list to indicate my sex. Balliol made me a present of books in recognition - as an inscription in one of them states - of my having gained in the Oxford Local examinations a distinction which would have entitled me to an exhibition at Balliol College - a good instance of a suppressed protasis. Worcester took a bolder course. It had advertised an Exhibition of £70 a year tenable during residence for four years under the following conditions :

It shall be offered to those Senior Candidates successively who shall obtain the highest place in the First Division of the General List provided they were placed in the First Division of one at least of the four first sections of the Examination. Testimonials of character required.

I had fulfilled these conditions, and my father (J. E. Thorold Rogers) received the following letter:

Worcester College
Oxford.

Dear Professor Rogers,

I don't know whether the name of the person who heads the Local Examination list is that of a member of your family. Should it be so, may I ask you to communicate to the candidate in question the offer of an exhibition at Worcester College on the part of the Provost and Fellows in accordance with the notice of last February?

Believe me,
Yours sincerely,
C. Henry Daniel,

Aug. 23. 1873   Tutor.

The question of opening the University to women was thus raised for the first time, and I may claim to be the *fons et origo mali* of the admission of women to the University, if a *malum* it was.

The matter was not pressed. My father wrote to the *Daily News* (Oct. 28, 1873) and after referring to Mr. Daniel's letter he added:

A correspondence under these circumstances was held between the Vice-Chancellor and myself - I urging that in my opinion the Statutes of the University do not debar the Vice-Chancellor from matriculating women and admitting them to the examinations which are at present only sought by men ; and the Vice-Chancellor, very naturally, requiring me to supply him with a case in which the question of his power could be raised. This I have for very obvious reasons declined to do because I think that the grant or refusal of a common law right, that of admission, under certain circumstances of proficiency, to one of the two ancient Universities, should not be raised on an isolated case, and from a natural dislike to invite the inevitable publicity to one's daughter which the ventilation of such a case would involve.

The college eventually awarded the Exhibition to a boy who was sixth in the list.

The beginnings of women's education in Oxford

Lady Margaret Hall and Somerville College, 1879

Lady Margaret and Somerville, which owed their existence to Committees constituted in 1878, were opened in October 1879, the one with ten students, the other with eleven. They had financial backing, but no benefaction on a large scale for more than forty years. The expense of administration, owing largely to the unpaid work done by Oxford residents and the willingness of the Principals to accept very small salaries, was inconsiderable. Their students were not all poor, but the standard of living for women of the class to which most of them belonged was simple. They had no organized games and few amusements or facilities for entertaining or being entertained by junior members of the University. Dances in Oxford were almost out of the question, and chaperonage was strict. My mother, for instance, was not allowed to chaperon to my brother's rooms a pupil of my own who was quite ten years his senior. The life at Lady Margaret was to be that of a 'Christian family', at Somerville that of an 'English family'.

St. Hugh's College, 1886
In 1886 Miss Wordsworth founded St. Hugh's Hall (now College) . . . Finding that she had about £600 as her share of a guarantee fund for the foundation of the Bishopric of Southwell, to which her father, then Bishop of Lincoln, had contributed, but which was not called up, she resolved to try the experiment of a hall of a rather less expensive character than Lady Margaret. She looked upon it as a tribute to her father and gave it the name of St. Hugh, Bishop of Lincoln (1186 - 1200).

St. Hilda's College, 1893
St. Hilda's was founded by Miss Dorothea Beale, Principal of the Ladies College, Cheltenham... Her object, as explained in a paper written for the *Cheltenham Ladies College Magazine* (Spring 1893), was to establish a hostel in which the best Cheltenham scholars who had done well in examinations should have a year in which, as she put it, 'They should be allowed to expatiate in intellectual pastures in a way in which we older women used to do before examinations for women existed'.

If Miss Davies and Miss Clough could have known!

THE TIMES, OCTOBER 31, 1971

Cambridge To Have New Mixed College

From Our Correspondent
Cambridge, Oct 31

An anonymous benefactor has agreed to found the first coeducational undergraduate college at Cambridge University. Fellows of Gonville and Caius College have agreed in principle to his request to make available a piece of their land for the college.

A statement from Gonville and Caius said that for some time the college had been considering a plan to found an independent coresidential and mainly undergraduate college in the city.

Dr. Joseph Needham, the Master of Caius, said he could not recall another case in the history of the university where a college had been helped so magnificently to generate another college. He expected the problems of location, architecture and planning of the new college to be solved within five years, although he could not say when the college would be in operation. It would be "an average-sized Cambridge college" with about 300 undergraduates of mixed sexes, about fifty research students and a fellowship body of about forty, again with the sexes equally mixed. There was a likelihood that the college would alternate with a master and a mistress.

The benefactor, Dr. Needham added, was "extremely tenacious" in maintaining his anonymity, although he thought he would reveal himself in time.

There is a move in Cambridge to bring women undergraduates into a number of men's colleges. Graduate colleges and societies are already coeducational, but this will be the first time that an undergraduate college has been founded along coeducational lines.

9

THE WRITERS

ST. TERESA OF AVILA

I have, as it were, to steal the time and that with difficulty,
because my writing hinders me from spinning. I am living in a
house that is poor and have many things to do.

*   *   *

JANE AUSTEN, 1775 - 1817

Sense and Sensibility, 1811

"A woman of seven and twenty," said Marianne, after pausing
a moment, "can never hope to feel or inspire affection again,
and if her home be uncomfortable, or her fortune small, I can
suppose that she might bring herself to submit to the offices of
a nurse, for the sake of the provision and security of a wife. In
his marrying such a woman, therefore, there would be nothing
unsuitable. It would be a compact of convenience, and the
world would be satisfied. In my eyes, it would be no marriage
at all, but that would be nothing. To me it would seem only a
commercial exchange, in which each wished to be benefited at
the expense of the other."

Correspondence with Crosbie & Co., publishers, concerning Northanger Abbey MS ("Susan")

To Crosbie & Co. (Wednesday) 5 April 1809 (JA's copy)

Gentlemen
In the spring of the year 1803 a MS Novel in 2 vol. entitled Susan was sold to you by a Gentleman of the name of Seymour, & the purchase money £10 recd at the same time. Six years have since passed, & this work of which I am myself the Authoress, has never to the best of my knowledge, appeared in print, tho' an early publication was stipulated for at the time of sale. I can only account for such an extraordinary circumstance by supposing the MS. by some carelessness to have been lost; & if that was the case, am willing to supply you with another copy if you are disposed to avail yourselves of it, & will engage for no farther delay when it comes into your hands. It will not be in my power from particular circumstances to command this copy before the Month of August, but then, if you accept my proposal, you may depend on receiving it. Be so good as to send me a Line in answer as soon as possible, as my stay in this place will not exceed a few days. Should no notice be taken of this address, I shall feel myself at liberty to secure the publication of my work, by applying elsewhere. I am Gentlemen &c. &c.
April 5. 1809.   M.A.D.

Direct to Mrs. Ashton Dennis
        Post Office, Southampton

From Richard Crosby. (Saturday) 8 April, 1809

Madam
We have to acknowledge the receipt of your letter of the 5th inst. It is true that at the time mentioned we purchased of Mr. Seymour a MS. novel entitled *Susan* and paid him for it the sum of 10£ for which we have his stamped receipt as a full consideration, but there was not any time stipulated for its publication, neither are we bound to publish it. Should you or

71

anyone else *(sic)* we shall take proceedings to stop the sale. The MS. shall be yours for the same as we paid for it.

For R. Crosby & Co.,

I am yours etc.,

Richard Crosby

London,
Ap 8 1809.

Emma, 1816

After a mutual silence of some minutes, Harriet thus began again—"I do so wonder, Miss Woodhouse, that you should not be married, or going to be married! so charming as you are!"—

Emma laughed, and replied,

"My being charming, Harriet, is not quite enough to induce me to marry; I must find other people charming—one other person at least. And I am not only, not going to be married, at present, but have very little intention of ever marrying at all."

"Ah! so you say; but I cannot believe it."

"I must see somebody very superior to any one I have seen yet, to be tempted; Mr. Elton, you know, (recollecting herself), is out of the question: and I do *not* wish to see any such person. I would rather not be tempted. I cannot really change for the better. If I were to marry, I must expect to repent it."

"Dear me!—it is so odd to hear a woman talk so!"—

"I have none of the usual inducements of women to marry. Were I to fall in love, indeed, it would be a different thing! but I never have been in love; it is not my way, or my nature; and I do not think I ever shall. And, without love, I am sure I should be a fool to change such a situation as mine. Fortune I do not want; employment I do not want; consequence I do not want: I believe few married women are half as much mistress of their husband's house, as I am of Hartfield; and never, never, could I expect to be so truly beloved and important; so always first and always right in any man's eyes as I am in my father's."

"But then, to be an old maid at last, like Miss Bates!"

"That is as formidable an image as you could present, Harriet; and if I thought I should ever be like Miss Bates! so silly—so satisfied—so smiling—so prosing—so undistinguishing and unfastidious—and so apt to tell everything relative to everybody about me, I would marry tomorrow. But between *us*, I am convinced there never can be any likeness, except in being unmarried."

"But still, you will be an old maid! and that's so dreadful!"

"Never mind, Harriet, I shall not be a poor old maid; and it is poverty only which makes celibacy contemptible to a generous public! A single woman, with a very narrow income, must be a ridiculous, disagreeable old maid! the proper sport of boys and girls; but a single woman, of good fortune, is always respectable, and may be as sensible and pleasant as anybody else. And the distinction is not quite so much against the candour and common sense of the world as appears at first; for a very narrow income has a tendency to contract the mind, and sour the temper. Those who can barely live, and who live perforce in a very small, and generally very inferior, society, may well be illiberal and cross . . .

"Dear me! but what shall you do? how shall you employ yourself when you grow old?"

"If I know myself, Harriet, mine is an active, busy mind, with a great many independent resources; and I do not perceive why I should be more in want of employment at forty or fifty than one-and-twenty."

Jane Austen to her niece, Fanny Knight

Thursday 20 Feb. (1817)
Chawton Feb. 20

My dearest Fanny,

You are inimitable, irresistable. You are the delight of my Life. Such Letters, such entertaining Letters as you have lately sent! Such a description of your queer little heart! Such a lovely display of what Imagination does. You are worth your weight in Gold, or even in the new Silver Coinage. I cannot express to you what I have felt in reading your history of yourself, how full of Pity & Concern & Admiration & Amusement I have been. You are the Paragon of all that is Silly & Sensible, common-place & eccentric, Sad and Lively, Provoking & Interesting. Who can keep pace with the fluctuations of your Fancy, the Capprizios of your Taste, the Contradictions of your Feelings? You are so odd! - & all the time so perfectly natural - so peculiar in yourself, & yet so like everybody else!

It is very, very gratifying to me to know you so intimately. You can hardly think what a pleasure it is to me, to have such thorough pictures of your Heart. Oh! what a loss it will be when you are married. You are too agreable in your single state, too agreable as a Neice. I shall hate you when your delicious play of Mind is all settled down into conjugal & maternal affections.

Mr. J.W. frightens me. He will have you. I see you at the Altar. I have *some* faith in Mrs. C. Cage's observation, & still more in Lizzy's; & besides, I know it *must* be so. He must be wishing to attach you. It would be too stupid & too shameful in him, to be otherwise; & all the Family are seeking your acquaintance.

Do not imagine that I have any real objection, I have rather taken a fancy to him than not, & I like Chilham Castle for you; I only do not like you shd marry anybody. And yet I do wish you to marry very much, because I know you will never be happy till you are; but the loss of a Fanny Knight will be never made up to me; My "affec: Neice F. C. Wildman" will be but a poor Substitute....

✳   ✳   ✳

CHARLOTTE BRONTË, 1816-1855

Concerning Miss Harriet Martineau, economist and novelist, 1802 - 1876

To Ellen Nussey, December 18th, 1850

The Knoll,Ambleside,
December 18th, 1850.

Dear Ellen,
. . .

I am better now. I am at Miss Martineau's for a week. Her house is very pleasant, both within and without; arranged at all points with admirable neatness and comfort. Her visitors enjoy the most perfect liberty; what she claims for herself she allows them. I rise at my own hour, breakfast alone (she is up at five, and takes a cold bath, and a walk by starlight, and has finished breakfast and got to her work by seven o'clock). I pass the morning in the drawing-room, she in her study. At two o'clock we meet; work, talk, and walk together till five, her dinner-hour; spend the evening together, when she converses fluently and abundantly, and with the most complete frankness. I go to my own room soon after ten; she sits up writing letters till twelve. She appears exhaustless in strength and spirits, and indefatigable in the faculty of labour. She is a great and a good woman; of course not without peculiarities, but I have seen none as yet that annoy me. She is both hard and warm-hearted, abrupt and affectionate, liberal and despotic. I believe she is not at all conscious of her own absolutism. When I tell her of it, she denies the charge warmly; then I laugh at her. I believe she almost rules Ambleside. Some of the gentry dislike her, but the lower orders have a great regard for her. I will not stay more than a week because about Christmas relatives and guests will come. Sir J. and Lady Shuttleworth are coming here to dine on Thursday. Write to me and say how you are. Kind regards to all.—Yours faithfully,

C. Brontë

*　　*　　*

MRS. ELIZABETH CLEGHORN GASKELL, 1810 -1865

Ruth, 1853

Sally tells of her Sweethearts
But Ruth said she would rather hear about Sally's sweethearts; much to the disappointment of the latter, who considered the dinner by far the greatest achievement.
"Well, you see, I don't know as I should call them sweethearts; for excepting John Rawson, who was shut up in a mad-house the next week, I never had what you may call a downright offer of marriage but once. But I had once; and so I may say I had a sweetheart. I was beginning to be afeard though, for one likes to be axed; that's but civility; and I remember, after I had turned forty, and afore Jeremiah Dixon

75

had spoken, I began to think John Rawson had perhaps not been so very mad, and that I'd done ill to lightly his offer, as a madman's, if it was to be the only one I was ever to have; I don't mean as I'd have had him, but I thought, if it was to come o'er again, I'd speak respectful of him to folk, and say it were only his way to go about on all-fours, but that he was a sensible man in most things. However, I'd had my laugh, and so had others, at my crazy lover, and it was late now to set him up as a Solomon. However, I thought it would be no bad thing to be tried again; but I little thought the trial would come when it did. You see, Saturday night is a leisure night in counting-houses and such-like places, while it's the busiest of all for servants. Well! it was a Saturday night, and I'd my baize apron on, and the tails of my bed-gown pinned together behind, down on my knees, pipeclaying the kitchen, when a knock comes to the back door. 'Come in!' says I; but it knocked again, as if it were too stately to open the door for itself; so I got up rather cross, and opened the door; and there stood Jerry Dixon, Mr. Holt's head-clerk; only he was not head-clerk then. So I stood, stopping up the door, fancying he wanted to speak to master; but he kind of pushed past me, and telling me summut about the weather (as if I could not see it for myself), he took a chair, and sat down by the oven. 'Cool and easy!' thought I; meaning hisself, not his place, which I knew must be pretty hot. Well! it seemed no use standing waiting for my gentleman to go; not that he had much to say either; but he kept twirling his hat round and round, and smoothing the nap on't with the back of his hand. So at last I squatted down to my work, and thinks I, I shall be on my knees all ready if he puts up a prayer, for I knew he was a Methodee by bringing-up, and had only lately turned to master's way of thinking; and them Methodees are terrible hands at unexpected prayers when one least looks for 'em. I can't say I like their way of taking one by surprise, as it were; but then I'm a parish-clerk's daughter, and could never demean myself to dissenting fashions, always save and except Master Thurstan's, bless him. However, I'd been caught once or twice unawares, so this time I thought I'd be up to it, and I moved a dry duster wherever I went, to kneel upon in case he began when I were in a wet place. By-and-by I thought, if the man would pray it would be a blessing, for it would prevent his sending his eyes after me wherever I went; for when they takes to praying they shuts their eyes, and quivers th' lids in a queer kind o' way—them Dissenters does. I can speak pretty plain to you, for you're bred in the Church like mysel', and must find it as out o' the way as I do to be among dissenting folk. God forbid I should speak disrespectful of Master Thurstan and Miss Faith, though; I never think on them as Church or Dissenters, but just as Christians. But to come back to Jerry. First, I tried always to be cleaning at his back; but when he wheeled round, so as always to face me, I thought I'd try a different game. So, says I, 'Master Dixon, I ax your pardon, but I must pipeclay under your chair. Will you please to move?' Well, he moved; and by-and-by I was at him again with the same words; and at after that, again and again, till he were always moving about wi' his chair behind him, like a snail as carries its house on its back. And the great gaupus never seed that I were pipeclaying the same places twice over. At last I got desperate cross, he were so in my way; so I made two big crosses on the tails of his brown coat; for you see, wherever he went, up or down, he drew out the tails of his coat from under him, and stuck them through the bars of the chair; and flesh and blood could not resist pipeclaying them for him; and a pretty brushing he'd have, I reckon, to get it off again. Well! at length he clears his throat uncommon loud; so I spreads my duster, and shuts my eyes all ready; but when nought comed of it, I opened my eyes a little bit to see what he were about. My word! if there he wasn't down on his knees right facing me, staring as hard as he could. Well! I thought it would be hard work to stand that, if he made a long ado; so I shut my eyes again, and tried to think serious, as became what I fancied were coming; but forgive me! but I thought why couldn't the fellow go in and pray wi' Master Thurstan, as had always a calm spirit ready for prayer, instead o' me who had my dresser to scour, let alone an apron to iron. At last he says, says he, 'Sally! will you oblige me with your hand?' So I thought it were, maybe, Methodee fashion to pray hand in hand ; and I'll not deny but I wished I'd washed it better after blackleading the kitchen fire. I thought I'd better tell him it were not so clean as I could wish, so says I, 'Master Dixon, you shall have it and welcome, if I may just go and wash 'em first.' But, says he, 'My dear Sally, dirty or clean, it's all the same to me, seeing I'm only speaking in a figuring way. What I'm asking on my bended knees is, that you'd please be so kind as

77

to be my wedded wife; week after next will suit me, if it's agreeable to you!' My word! I were up on my feet in an instant! It were odd now, weren't it? I never thought of taking the fellow, and getting married; for all, I'll not deny, I had been thinking it would be agreeable to be axed. But all at once, I couldn't abide the chap. 'Sir,' says I, trying to look shamefaced as became the occasion, but for all that feeling a twittering round my mouth that I were afeard might end in a laugh - 'Master Dixon, I'm obleeged to you for the compliment, and thank ye all the same, but I think I'd prefer a single life.' He looked mighty taken aback; but in a minute he cleared up, and was as sweet as ever. He still kept on his knees, and I wished he'd take himself up; but I reckon, he thought it would give force to his words; says he, 'Think again, my dear Sally. I've a four-roomed house, and furniture conformable; and eighty pounds a year. You may never have such a chance again.' There were truth enough in that, but it was not pretty in the man to say it; and it put me up a bit. 'As for that, neither you nor I can tell, Master Dixon. You're not the first chap as I've had down on his knees afore me, axing me to marry him (you see I were thinking of John Rawson, only I thought there were no need to say he were on all-fours-it were truth he were on his knees, you know), and maybe you'll not be the last. Anyhow I've no wish to change my condition just now.' 'I'll wait till Christmas,' says he. 'I've a pig as will be ready for killing then, so I must get married before that.' Well now! would you believe it? the pig was a temptation. I'd a receipt for curing hams, as Miss Faith would never let me try saying the old way were good enough. However, I resisted. Says I, very stern, because I felt I'd been wavering. 'Master Dixon, once and for all, pig or no pig, I'll not marry you. And if you'll take my advice, you'll get up off your knees. The flags is but damp yet, and it would be an awkward thing to have rheumatiz just before winter.' With that he got up, stiff enough. He looked as sulky a chap as ever I clapped eyes on. And as he were so black and cross, I thought I'd done well (whatever came of the pig) to say 'No' to him. 'You may live to repent this,' says he, very red. 'But I'll not be hard upon ye, I'll give you another chance. I'll let you have the night to think about it, and I'll just call in to hear your second thoughts, after chapel tomorrow.' Well now! did ever you hear the like! But that is the way with all of them

78

men, thinking so much of themselves, and that it's but ask and have. They've never had me, though; and I shall be sixty-one next Martinmas, so there's not much time left for them to try me, I reckon. Well! when Jeremiah said that he put me up more than ever, and I says, 'My first thoughts, second thoughts, and third thoughts is all one and the same; you've but tempted me once, and that was when you spoke of your pig. But of yoursel' you're nothing to boast on, and so I'll bid you good night, and I'll keep my manners, or else, if I told the truth, I should say it had been a great loss of time talking to you. But I'll be civil - so good night.' He never said a word, but went off as black as thunder, slamming the door after him. The master called me into prayers, but I can't say I could put my mind to them for my heart was beating so. However, it was a comfort to have had an offer of holy matrimony; and though it flustered me, it made me think more of myself. In the night, I began to wonder if I'd not been cruel and hard to him. You see, I were feverish-like; and the old song of Barbary Allen would keep running in my head, and I thought I were Barbary, and he were young Jemmy Gray, and that maybe he'd die for love of me; and I pictured him to mysel', lying on his death-bed, with his face turned to the wall, 'wi' deadly sorrow sighing,' and I could ha' pinched mysel' for having been so like cruel Barbary Allen. And when I got up next day, I found it hard to think on the real Jerry Dixon I had seen the night before, apart from the sad and sorrowful Jerry I thought on a-dying, when I were between sleeping and waking. And for many a day I turned sick, when I heard the passing bell, for I thought it were the bell loud-knelling which were to break my heart wi' a sense of what I'd missed in saying 'No' to Jerry, and so killing him with cruelty. But in less than a three week, I heard parish bells a-ringing merrily for a wedding; and in the course of the morning, some one says to me, 'Hark! how the bells is ringing for Jerry Dixon's wedding!' And, all on a sudden, he changed back again from a heart-broken young fellow like Jemmy Gray, into a stout, middle-aged man, ruddy complexioned, with a wart on his left cheek like life!''

*　　*　　*

ADELAIDE ANNE PROCTER, 1825 - 1864

Legends and Lyrics and other Poems, 1858

Returned - "Missing"
(Five Years After)

> Yes, I was sad and anxious,
> But now, dear, I am gay;
> I know that it is wisest
> To put all hope away:—
> Thank God that I have done so
> And can be calm to-day.
>
> For hope deferred - you know it,
> Once made my heart so sick:
> Now, I expect no longer;
> It is but the old trick
> Of hope, that makes me tremble,
> And makes my heart beat quick.
>
> All day I sit here calmly;
> Not as I did before,
> Watching for one whose footstep
> Comes never, never more . . .
> Hush! was that some one passing,
> Who paused beside the door?
>
> For years I hung on chances,
> Longing for just one word;
> At last I feel it:—silence
> Will never more be stirred . . .
> Tell me once more that rumour,
> You fancied you had heard.
>
> Life has more things to dwell on
> Than just one useless pain,
> Useless and past for ever;
> But noble things remain,
> And wait us all: . . . you too, dear,
> Do you think hope quite vain?

All others have forgotten,
'Tis right I should forget,
Nor live on a keen longing
Which shadows forth regret:
Are not the letters coming?
The sun is almost set.

Now that my restless legion
Of hopes and fears is fled,
Reading is joy and comfort . . .
. . . This very day I read,
Oh, such a strange returning
Of one whom all thought dead!

Not that *I* dream or fancy,
You know all that is past;
Earth has no hope to give me,
And yet:—Time flies so fast
That all but the impossible
Might be brought back at last.

*   *   *

CHRISTINA ROSSETTI, 1830 - 1894

From "Valentines to my Mother", 1847

My blessed Mother dozing in her chair
On Christmas Day seemed an embodied Love,
A comfortable Love with soft brown hair
Softened and silvered to a tint of dove;
A better sort of Venus with an air
Angelical from thoughts that dwell above;
A wiser Pallas in whose body fair
Enshrined a blessed soul looks out thereof.
Winter brought holly then; now Spring has brought
Paler and frailer snowdrops shivering!
And I have brought a simple humble thought—
I her devoted duteous Valentine—
A lifelong thought which thrills this song I sing,
A lifelong love to this dear Saint of mine.

81

"No, Thank You, John"

I never said I loved you, John:
Why will you tease me day by day,
And wax a weariness to think upon
With always "do" and "pray"?

You know I never loved you, John;
No fault of mine made me your toast:
Why will you haunt me with a face as wan
As shows an hour-old ghost?

I dare say Meg or Moll would take
Pity on you, if you'd ask:
And pray don't remain single for my sake
Who can't perform that task.

I have no heart?—Perhaps I have not;
But then you're mad to take offence
That I don't give you what I have not got:
Use your own common sense.

Let bygones be bygones:
Don't call me false, who owed not to be true:
I'd rather answer "No" to fifty Johns
Than answer "Yes" to you.

Let's mar our pleasant days no more,
Song-birds of passage, days of youth:
Catch at to-day, forget the days before:
I'll wink at your untruth.

Let us strike hands as hearty friends;
No more, no less; and friendship's good:
Only don't keep in view ulterior ends,
And points not understood

Baroness Seear

Rev. R. Mary Webster

Dame Flora Robson, D.B.E.

Queen Elizabeth I,
painted by an unknown artist

Florence Nightingale

Chief Vestal Virgin

In open treaty. Rise above
Quibbles and shuffling off and on:
Here's friendship for you if you like; but love,—
No, thank you, John.

*   *   *

10

THE PIONEERS

FRANCES MARY BUSS

The terrible sufferings of the women of my own class for want of a good elementary training have more than ever intensified my earnest desire to lighten, ever so little, the misery of women brought up "to be married and taken care of" and left alone in the world destitute. It is impossible for words to express my fixed determination of alleviating this evil - even to the small extent of one neighbourhood only.

*   *   *

FLORENCE NIGHTINGALE, 1820 - 1910

Cassandra
Written 1852, privately printed 1859, published 1928

Family Pressures
The family uses people, *not* for what they are, nor for what they are intended to be, but for what it wants them for - its own uses. It thinks of them not as what God has made, but as the something which it has arranged that they shall be. If it wants someone to sit in the drawing-room, *that* someone is supplied by the family, though that member may be destined for science, or for education, or for active superintendence by God, *i.e.* by the gifts within.
This system dooms some minds to incurable infancy, others to silent misery.

And family boasts that it has performed its mission well, in as far as it has enabled the individual to say "I have *no* peculiar work, nothing but what the moment brings me, nothing that I cannot throw up at once at anybody's claim"; in as far, that is, as it has *destroyed* the individual life. And the individual thinks that a great victory has been accomplished, when, at last, she is able to say that she has "no personal desires or plans." What is this but throwing the gifts of God aside as worthless, and substituting for them those of the world?

Marriage is the only chance (and it is but a chance) offered to women for escape from this death; and how eagerly and how ignorantly it is embraced!

The process leading to marriage

But is it surprising that there should be so little real marriage, when we think what the process is which leads to marriage? Under the eyes of an always present mother and sisters (of whom even the most refined and intellectual cannot abstain from a jest upon the subject, who think it their *duty* to be anxious, to watch every germ and bud of it) the acquaintance begins. It is fed - upon what? - the gossip of art, musical and pictorial, the party politics of the day, the chit-chat of society, and people marry or sometimes they don't marry, discouraged by the impossiblity of knowing any more of one another than this will furnish.

They prefer to marry in *thought,* to hold imaginary conversations with one another in idea, rather than, on such a flimsy pretext of communion, to take the chance (certainty it cannot be) of having more to say to one another in marriage.

How to become acquainted?

Unless a woman had lost all pride, how is it possible for her, under the eyes of all her family, to indulge in long exclusive conversations with a man? "Such a thing" must not take place till after her "engagement." And how is she to make an engagement, if "such a thing" has not taken place?

Besides, young women at home have so little to occupy and to interest them - they have so little reason for *not* quitting their home, that a young and independent man cannot look at a girl without giving rise to "expectations" if not on her own part, on that of her family. Happy he, if he is not said to have been "trifling with her feelings," or "disappointing her hopes!"

Under these circumstances, how can a man, who has any pride or principle, become acquainted with a woman in such a manner as to *justify* them in marrying?

CECIL WOODHAM-SMITH

Florence Nightingale, 1950

One of the extraordinary features of Miss Nightingale's life is the passage of time. She starts with a "call" in 1837. But what has she been called to do? What is her vocation to be? Eight years pass before, in 1845, she finds out. Even then she is only half-way. Eight more years pass before she gains freedom in 1853 to pursue her vocation. Sixteen years in all, sixteen years during which the eager susceptible girl was slowly hammered into the steely powerful woman of genius . . .
Early in April 1853 Liz Herbert wrote that through Lady Canning she had heard of what might prove a suitable opening. The Institution for the care of Sick Gentlewomen in Distressed Circumstances, described by Miss Nightingale as "a Sanitarium for Sick Governesses run by a Committee of Fine Ladies", had got itself into difficulties. It was to be reorganised and moved from its premises in Chandos Street. The committee, of which Lady Canning was chairman, were looking for a Superintendent to undertake the reorganisation. Liz Herbert suggested Florence and Lady Canning, after consulting her committee, wrote describing the post and its requirements . . .
On April 18th there was an interview, and Lady Canning wrote the same day to Mrs. Herbert: 'I write a line in great haste to say that I was delighted with Miss N's quiet sensible manner. In one short acquaintance I am sure she must be a most remarkable person . . .'
When the news was broken to Fanny and Parthe sickeningly familiar scenes took place. Parthe wept, raged, worked herself into frenzy, collapsed and had to be put to bed. Fanny stormed, lamented and had to be given sal volatile. Meals were sent away untouched. Ordinary life was at an end. W. E. N. took refuge in the Athenaeum . . .
Miss Nightingale was not what her committee had expected. Her genius was of an unromantic character. She perceived that

unorganised devotion, unorganised self-sacrifice were useless. To bring about the installation of a row of bells "with valves that flew open" when the patient called was more effectual than to turn oneself into a devoted nurse, toiling endlessly up and down stairs because no such bells existed. To put in the best possible kitchen stove, to descend into the coal cellar and rake over the coal to ensure the coal merchant had not delivered an undue proportion of dust, to check stores and linen and provide patients with clean beds and good food were more effectual than to sit through the watches of the night cheering the dying moments of the patient expiring from scurvy and bed sores. But it was not so picturesque . . .

She was in tremendous spirits. On October 20th she wrote Fanny a letter, which was bursting with gaiety, asking for a pair of comfortable old boots - she was spending all day and most of the night on her feet: "Oh my boots! My boots! dearer to me than the best French polished, my brother boots. Where are ye, my boots. I never shall see your pretty faces more. My dear I *must* have them boots. . . . More flowers, more game, more grapes.". . .

The summer of 1854 marked the end of a chapter. The long agonising apprenticeship was over and the instrument uniquely fitted for its purpose was forged. In the world outside Harley Street a catastrophe was taking place. In March 1854 England and France had declared war on Russia. In September the Allied armies landed in the Crimea. Harley Street, with its unreasonable committee, its "deficient" saucepans, its ragged linen, had been a dress rehearsal. Now the curtain was about to go up on the play.

*   *   *

JO MANTON

Sister Dora: The Life of Dorothy Pattison, 1971
Dorothy Pattison - Sister Dora, 1832 - 1878

"An overpowering claim"
While Mrs. Pattison dragged out her weary invalid's existence,
her daughter could never leave home. It was not even that she
loved her mother greatly; the compulsion to serve was stronger
than ordinary affection . . . Nevertheless she did not, apart
from one attempt, consider leaving her mother to be nursed by
anyone else. Just so twenty years later, Florence Nightingale,
after years of fame and independence, returned to care for the
blind and senile mother with whom she had been in conflict
since girlhood. To such women helplessness and suffering
presented an overpowering claim.

*"Dorothy Pattison's life was ending; Sister Dora was about to
take her place"*
In January 1862 Dorothy Pattison was thirty. In looks and
bearing she appeared more like a girl of twenty, and to
outward view she had led a life sheltered from the world. In
fact she had passed through experiences that steeled her for
the best and the worst life had to offer. These experiences were
largely unknown to her contemporaries and have remained
unrecorded and unaccounted for until now. As a child she had
wandered untaught through a landscape of matchless poetry
and power. Below the surface respectability of Victorian
provincial life, she had seen madness, hatred, revenge,
suffering and death. She had known the angry bitterness of
religious strife and questioned her own faith to its
foundations. An ignorant girl, she had been guided in reading
and conversation by one of the most distinguished minds of
the day, and suffered the shock of rejection when she fell from
Mark's favour. She had felt the frustration of talents and
energies rusting unused, while the years passed by in deadly
sameness. She had been youthfully loved and in love, learning
too late the double-edged and dangerous power this gave her.
She had fought and won the battle for personal freedom.
Gradually under the stresses of life, the circle of family and
friendship broke. The scenery of her youth became, in Mark's

words, "the shell in which home love once was, and *is* no longer". She was now quite alone. Dorothy Pattison's life was ending; Sister Dora was about to take her place.

"Her was the best woman that ever cut a loaf"
Dora's character, and her supposedly miraculous powers, made her in the Black Country a legend like Florence Nightingale. A cult grew around her, as round a local saint in the Middle Ages. Her relics, a cup, a glove, a letter, a nurse's belt or scissors were treasured for years by their owners. Her picture hung in the place of honour in countless Walsall homes. Even the children shared in this feeling; a schoolmaster was amused and touched to see "how little ragged dirty urchins playing in the streets would run up as she walked along, pulling at her gown to attract her attention and not satisfied till she had bent down from her majestic height to kiss their grimy faces, which they held up to her with utter confidence". She could not have been so loved if all her powers had been devoted, as Mark Pattison claimed, to self-glorification. Was she really the remote aristocratic figure of her legend, "with whom none could ever venture to take a liberty, who worked without in the least descending from her social position"? . . .

The final comment comes from an anonymous patient, who was evidently a man of few, but very well chosen words. When asked his opinion of Sister Dora, he said, "Well, I have a leg more than I would have had, if it hadn't been for her." After a pause for thought he added, "Her was the best woman that ever cut a loaf." It would be simple but too shallow to say that these people loved Dora because she was an attractive and amusing person, or that they realized the rarity of her skill. Extreme suffering sweeps away the common, surface standards of judgment; anyone who has ever known great pain or fear can recall the anguish of isolation they impose, the rigid despair which stares out from concentration camp photographs. Sister Dora, from some depths of her nature, drew the power to enter this desolation. When she was there, patients, even those at the point of death, no longer felt themselves alone, face to face with the enemy. Her power was love, which the patients tested in matters of life and death,

89

and always found steadfast. They were inarticulate people, but they could feel, with Othello:

> *She loved me for the dangers I had passed;*
> *And I loved her that she did pity them.*

*　　*　　*

E. MOBERLY　BELL, 1881 - 1967

Octavia Hill, 1838 - 1912, published 1942

Accepts her Father's Debts
By this time Octavia had come to realize the true condition of her father's affairs. There were debts, she discovered, still unpaid, and although she had of course no legal responsibility for these (since her father was a discharged bankrupt) the idea that anyone should suffer loss through her family was utterly intolerable to her. With a full recognition of the burden she was assuming she accepted the debts as hers, and thereafter they figured as a liability in any calculation she made of her financial position; bit by bit, as she was able, she reduced and finally paid off the whole sum, but it was a slow business, and in 1856 she saw herself submerged under a mountain of indebtedness. A further source of unhappiness was the sad state of depression into which her father had fallen. She felt it her duty to go and see him from time to time, and every visit added to the weight of her burden. "I have been with my father, and what that implies of desolation and despair, God the good Father alone knows."

Work in Housing Management begins
Gradually the hostility of the tenants softened. They got used to the short sturdy figure which appeared punctually on the expected day, whatever the weather, and moved resolutely and buoyantly across the sordid yards; almost reluctantly they were obliged to recognize the pluck which took her alone, after dark, into places where the police were accustomed to visit only in pairs.
It is a significant fact that though many of her tenants were of

the roughest and most lawless type, she was never molested or robbed as she walked through them her collected rent in her bag.

Presently they began to appreciate the even justice of her rule and the fact that she never went back on her word in the smallest particular, and when they discovered that she would never walk into their rooms uninvited, the obstructive foot was withdrawn from the door.

When this stage was reached, it was possible to attempt to secure the co-operation of the tenants.

Interest in the Women's University Settlement

In Southwark the question of settlements touched Octavia more nearly both because of its proximity to her own work and because it was a settlement for women. She was not predisposed in its favour, for she believed so passionately in family life, that a collection of women, living together without family ties or domestic duties, seemed to her unnatural if not positively undesirable. She believed the part-time voluntary worker, who was fulfilling obligations to her home and family, had something to give which no professional social worker could supply. She was therefore a little doubtful about the Women's University Settlement, Southwark, whose Committee she joined in 1889, "not because I have very much confidence in the beneficial result of large or many settlements of workers bound together by no family ties, with no natural connection with a district; but because their settlement is the practical outcome of a very large association, and because a small group of these, settled in the heart of the South London poor, may be of the greatest use."

Fight for the National Trust

In all this work Octavia's staunchest ally had been Sir Robert Hunter. . . As early as 1884 he had been convinced of the desirability of founding some corporation which could hold land and buildings in trust for the people, and had read a paper on the subject in Birmingham. Octavia was in full sympathy with the project, its importance was brought home to her in the following year when Mr. Evelyn, a Deptford landlord, wished to hand over to the people Sayes Court with its large garden and was unable to carry out his scheme in its entirety, because there was no public body able to hold both building and land. Octavia was convinced of the practicability of the scheme and discussed with Robert Hunter a suitable name for the proposed body: "A short expressive name," she wrote in February, 1885, "is difficult to find for the new Company. What do you think of the 'Commons and Gardens Trust' and then printing in small letters 'for accepting, holding, preserving and purchasing open spaces for the people in town and country.' I do not know that I am right in thinking that it should be called Trust, but I think it might be better than 'Company'. You will do better, I believe, to bring forward its benevolent than its commercial character. People don't like unsuccessful business, but do like charity when a little money goes a long way because of good commercial management." Across the letter Sir Robert scribbled in pencil "? National Trust".

Meetings were organized over which influential people presided, and there were distinguished speakers, but it was Octavia who held the audience and made an impression not easily effaced. Power flowed from her, for she spoke with an eloquence derived from her passionate belief in the gospel she was preaching. . .

When she spoke of the hills, the headlands, the commons, her hearers saw these through her eyes, and perhaps recaptured some happy memories of earlier and easier days. They were convinced of the importance of saving them for all time. She wrote articles, too, which were readily accepted and gradually the idea of the National Trust took root in many minds. . . .

Mrs. Fanny Talbot was its first benefactor giving to it the cliff at Barmouth. "We have got our first property," said Octavia to Sydney Cockerell with a smile, "I wonder whether it will be our last."

But she never for a moment believed it would be the last.

JOSEPHINE KAMM

Rapiers and Battleaxes, 1966

Mary Carpenter, 1807 - 1877

Work for children

For some years after she left school Mary continued to study, and in 1829 she and her mother opened a girls' school in Bristol. But teaching middle class girls did not satisfy the yearnings of a young woman who longed to be of use in the world. Her life was rooted in her religion, and her religion demanded of her service to the under-privileged. The starting-point of her career was a meeting with an American philanthropist, Dr. Joseph Tuckerman of Boston, who visited Bristol in 1833. He drew her attention to a wretched looking little boy who rushed out of a dark alleyway as they passed by in the street. That boy, remarked Dr. Tuckerman, ought to be followed to his home and something concrete done to help him.

From her childhood onwards Mary Carpenter had been known in the family as "motherly". So now, quite naturally, she gravitated towards work for the children of the poor. In 1835 she founded a Working and Visiting Society in Bristol and remained its secretary for twenty years; and when in 1846 she realized that nothing at all was being done for the so-called "gutter" children she started a "ragged" school in the Bristol slums. Her pupils were abjectly poor. Some were homeless and parentless; and the homes of the more fortunate were squalid in the extreme. The children formed a wild and lawless gang, unaccustomed to discipline of any kind. Some seemed mentally retarded; yet under their teacher's benign influence they made more progress than she had at first thought possible. It was an inspiring sight, wrote her friend, the stout, amusing suffragist and anti-vivisectionist Frances Power Cobbe (1822 - 1904), to watch her "teaching, singing, and praying with the wild streetboys, in spite of endless inter-ruptions caused by shooting marbles into hats on the table behind her, whistling, stamping, fighting, shrieking out 'Amen' in the middle of the prayer, and sometimes rising *en masse* and tearing, like a lot of bisons in hobnailed shoes, down from the gallery, round the great schoolroom , and down the stairs out into the street. These irrespressible outbreaks she bore with infinite good humour."

Good humour, patience, and love were the chief characteristics which Mary Carpenter brought to her work.

*   *   *

JOSEPHINE KAMM

Rapiers and Battleaxes, 1966

Louisa Twining, 1820 - 1912

Workhouse Reform

Running parallel with Mary Carpenter's work is the work of her near-contemporary Louisa Twining, the originator of Workhouse Reform. Louisa Twining was one of the nine children of a prosperous tea merchant, a scholarly man and a member of the Royal Society and the Society of Arts. Her home life was secure and happy, and there was no need for her to work; but she and her elder sister Elizabeth (1805 - 89) both felt they owed a debt to society. Elizabeth Twining, who wrote a number of religious and philanthropical books, organized mothers' meetings in London and was concerned in the establishment of Bedford College for women in 1849.

Louisa's career was with a lower stratum of society. She possessed the energy and drive of Mary Carpenter, together with a lively intelligence and a probing mind. She was drawn into district visiting by way of friendly calls on a retired nurse of the family who lived in the parish of St. Clement Danes. When she went to see the old nurse she sometimes called on her neighbours, and was shocked by the conditions in which they lived. But she was still more shocked by the state of the Strand Union Workhouse, to which one of these old people retired. In 1853 when Louisa Twining first saw it, the Strand Union was a noisome place. One of its drawbacks was a laundry in the cellars which filled the building from one week's end to the next with the steam and smells from the paupers' washing. Workhouse food was disgusting and totally inadequate: the wards were a jumble of the aged, the depraved and the drunken. There were no proper arrangements for nursing the sick, who were housed in rooms in the main building and cared for - when they were cared for at all - by elderly inmates who happened to be sufficiently sober at the time and could be bribed for their pains with beer and extra food. For laying out the dead and for specially unpleasant tasks a small glass of gin was expected as an additional bait. The mortality rate, especially among mothers and children, was appallingly high; while the combined sounds of carpet-beating which went on all day outside one of the men's wards, the tinker's shop which was situated outside another, and the women's insane ward immediately beneath the lying-in ward, effectively deprived the inmates of rest. Even worse than the physical conditions in Louisa Twining's eyes was the dreadful loneliness and monotony of the existence. Coffin and shroud-making was the only occupation of the inmates; and the frequent arrival of the parish hearse to remove a corpse the only break in the monotony.

The Strand Union was typical of the workhouses of the time: in some conditions were even more scandalous; yet no improvements or alleviations were thought necessary. Louisa Twining had quickly taken it on herself to go about among the 500 inmates of the Strand Union bringing small gifts with her. When, however, she applied to the Poor Law Guardians for permission to recruit a band of volunteers to help her she was curtly informed that voluntary efforts would endanger the discipline of the workhouse and create an inconvenient precedent. Undeterred by the rebuff, Louisa Twining put on her best bonnet and cloak and took a cab to Whitehall to interview the Guardians. She was extremely nervous a fact which was not lost on the hall-porter. "You need not be afraid, ma'am", he told her; "you will find they are very nice gentlemen indeed."

Kind they may well have been; but Louisa Twining had to nag at them for more than a year before they gave a reluctant consent to organized workhouse visiting, and then only on condition that it was carried out quietly and unobtrusively. As soon as the necessary permission had been obtained an orderly band of women turned up "carrying snuff, tobacco, tracts, hymn books, and spectacles to the aged poor". They were as quiet and unobtrusive as the Guardians could wish, but they kept their eyes wide open and once outside the workhouse they

95

were free to speak and write about the offensive conditions within.

In the meantime, Louisa Twining had written a paper on *The Conditions of our Workhouses* for the 1857 congress of the Social Science Association: it was the first time the subject was debated in public. She followed this up with a paper on *Workhouse Management* for the 1858 congress, and with letters and articles for the Press which attracted a great deal of notice and led to the formation of a proper Workhouse Visiting Society.

*   *   *

MARGARET WEDDELL, 1886 - 1958

Child Care Pioneers, 1958

Margaret McMillan, 1860 - 1931

Pioneer of Nursery Schools
Early in this century, fifty little children, aged five years, were sitting in raised tiers of seats, known as a gallery. Each child sat in the same position to commands of "Hands behind!" "Hands in front!" "Hands on head!" "Hands on books!" There was no freedom of movement, no choice of occupation. Ten years later, there was seen in Deptford, in a London slum, the beginnings of a garden. Children played happily about, singing, smelling the flowers, running or sitting or moving, each individually. There was colour and the scent of flowers in place of the fish-and-chips that reeked in the neighbouring streets. A school of a new type had begun. Our nursery and infant schools today are famous throughout the world. The one who led the way was Margaret McMillan.

Rachel and Margaret McMillan, the founders of the Nursery School Movement in Britain, were born in America, the children of a Scottish settler who hailed from Glen Urquhart in the Highlands. They had for five or six years a happy childhood in West Chester, about ten miles from New York. The garden was full of trees and flowers, and from the end of it they looked out on the waters of the estuary where the East and Hudson Rivers joined. The wooden house, built in Dutch fashion, seemed less a house than a "roofed series of gateways opening on the wide sunlit world." It was the time of the American Civil War, and in the fierce summer of 1865, their little sister Elizabeth, and then their father, died. Rachel had always been delicate and their mother was advised to return to Britain. But Margaret never forgot those early years and wanted for every child the joy of space, of sunshine on bare limbs, and of experiencing at first hand the changing lights of the daytime, and the varying glories of the seasons.

Mrs. McMillan went to her parents, the Camerons, who lived in Inverness, and there Rachel and Margaret spent the next ten years. They attended Inverness High School, their mother sparing nothing to give them a good education. At fifteen Rachel went for three years to a boarding school in Coventry and Margaret, after she was eighteen, spent some years abroad studying music at Frankfurt and as a governess teaching English and studying languages at Lausanne and Geneva. Meanwhile in Inverness, Rachel was spending a quiet and uneventful life, nursing her grandmother. The reading of Stead's articles *The Maiden Tribute* seems to have been a landmark in her life. She became aware of the dark world of unhappy girls and women beyond her sheltered circle, and on a visit in 1887 to her cousins in Edinburgh, was inspired by the new Socialism. She attended lectures, read pamphlets, and when her grandmother died in the summer of 1888, went to London as a helper in a working girls' home in Bloomsbury for a salary of £20 a year. It was she who gave her sister the first impulse to social work . . .

Margaret McMillan died in 1931. A fine memorial training college and school named after her now stands in Bradford, and the Rachel McMillan Training College stands on the original site in Deptford. The Nursery School Association, founded in 1923 with Margaret as President, exists to promote that early childhood training which experience taught her was what mattered most in education. The French educationalist who inspired her - Seguin - once wrote, in words she quoted, "How few children are allowed to remain, dreaming, touching, and handling things on the knees of their good mothers . . . and coming out of the baptism of emotion, thinkers, leaders and artists". Towards this ideal Margaret had devoted her life.

A. OLWEN CAMPBELL, 1889 - 1959

Mary Kingsley (1862 - 1900)
A Victorian in the Jungle, published 1957

The First Journey

One turns with an enormous feeling of relief and pleasure to Mary's years of freedom - years which she packed so full of activity, adventure and public service, and some of which she so much enjoyed. What she called "sky-larking in Africa", a sport which involved incredible discomforts as well as dangers, seems to have satisfied her nature as nothing else could have done. Here she found endless opportunities for exploring queer places and making queer friends, and for exercising her inexhaustible sense of humour and fun. The energies so long checked back, flowed out in a flood.

But the sahdow of the past remained with her. It is common enough for a biographer to lament the loss the world suffers when highly gifted men and women are cut off by early death. We seldom mourn - perhaps we can seldomer see - the damage or destruction of rare qualities, the toll taken of personality, no matter how strong, by unnatural frustrations in youth. We forget that the spirit may lose a limb as the body can.

Everything that Mary Kingsley did and felt in the years of her freedom was coloured by the experiences of those early years during which so much of what belonged to her rich nature and heredity had been stifled by demands made and opportunities refused. She had been in a peculiar way *depersonalized*, and the loss is ours as well as hers. She had come to feel that she did not matter, and that feeling was bound to separate her to some extent from her friends, as it does from her biographer. Beneath her spontaneity and candour there was an iron barrier of reserve - a reserve which was probably quite unconscious, for she sometimes complained of loneliness and of not being understood. The origin of this reserve was perhaps a strongly suppressed resentment at the merciless way she had been exploited by the parents she had loved and served so faithfully; by the father she had so generously understood, but who had never troubled to understand her.

At the period of her young life when she had needed to discover and develop some of her own personal urges and

HONOUR TO AGNETA FRANCES RAMSAY!
(CAMBRIDGE. JUNE, 1887.)

"SENIORA FAWCETT."

So to be entitled henceforth, as she is
Seniorer to the Senior Wrangler.

Octavia Hill, painted by J. S. Sargent

Dame Christabel Pankhurst

ideals, constant and absorbing claims had been made on her time, her pity, and her sense of responsibility for others. Apart from this drain on her feelings, her emotional life was starved. She may well have been temperamentally shy and critical, but this tendency can only have been increased by such great isolation from normal human contacts outside her home. And though she was so much immersed in family life, there is nothing to suggest that any of her family on their side reached out in sympathy and understanding to her. "Not one of my own people is interested in the smallest degree in what I do or think," she said in a letter to John Holt in 1898; the "own people" referred to here were not, apart from her brother, her immediate family, for her parents were long dead; but there is every reason for thinking that this had been the attitude to her from the first in her own family circle. . .

"Her remoteness was not due to lack of feeling"
It is not surprising that when at last she achieved a full life, though she could give warm and loyal friendship she could not give herself; she was in some ways unapproachable; irretrievably self-dependent and emotionally alone. "I have never been in love," she once said, "nor has anyone ever been in love with me."
In her sketch of her own life she writes: "My life has been one wholly without romance or variety in the proper sense of the word. . .Why this has been is perfectly clear; it arises from my having no personal individuality of my own whatsoever. I have always lived in the lives of other people, whose work was heavy for them; and apart from that I have lived a life of my own, strewn about among non-human things."
A still greater degree of diffidence and aloofness appears in a later passage of the letter in which she said:"I am no more a human being than a gust of wind is." She continues:
"It never occurs to me that I have any right to do anything more than now and then sit and warm myself at the fires of real human beings. I am grateful to them for letting me do this. I am fond of them, but I don't expect them to be fond of me, and it is just as well I don't - for there is not one of them who has ever cared for me apart from my services . . . I am no better than the human beings I deal with in the matter of feeling. When they are happy and comfortable and snug, I lose all interest in them - as well as they in me - it is quite

mutual, save that I have more reason to be grateful to them than they to me, for it is through them I know this most amusing human world; but it is the non-human world I belong to myself."

We have to pick our way carefully among these strange confessions: they cannot be accepted literally. A life which held, even if only for a few years, such original adventures experienced with so much zest, and which was enriched by so many and varied friendships, can hardly be regarded as without romance and variety. Nor can we agree with her that she lacked individuality, since her individuality cries aloud in all that she did and wrote. When she implies that she had no human side, no real bonds with other people, she is being unjust to them and to herself. She was greatly loved by many people during those last years of her life; and the ardour with which she fought for wiser and juster treatment of Africans came from a very human, compassionate heart. Her remoteness was not due to lack of feeling.

Essential equipment in 1893: skirt and husband

In her personal kit she took an old pair of her brother's trousers - the only contribution he is ever reported to have made to her felicity - and owing to ineradicable Victorian modesty, a skirt to wear over the top of them. That skirt proved however to be useful as well as modest. In one of the wildest regions which she traversed on her second journey she fell, she tells us, into a fifteen-foot deep game-trap, lined with spikes. "It is at these times," she comments, "that you realise the blessing of a good thick skirt. Had I paid heed to the advice of many people in England . . . and adopted masculine garments, I should have been spiked to the bone and done for. Whereas, save for a good many bruises, here I was with the fullness of my skirt tucked under me, sitting on nine ebony spikes some twelve inches long, in comparative comfort, howling lustily to be hauled out." One valuable article for her equipment she had to do without. When on her second voyage she was planning to explore the Rapids of the Ogowé River in a native canoe she had some difficulty with the French authorities. They did not approve of her crew of Igalwas, and they said that the only other woman, a French lady, who had visited the Rapids had her husband with her. Mary replied that neither the Royal Geographical Society's list, in their

Hints to Travellers, nor Messrs Silver in their elaborate lists of articles necessary for a traveller in tropical climates "made mention of husbands". Quite often she found she had to invent a husband to pacify the natives. It did not do when they asked "Where is he?" to answer that she had not got one. "I have tried it and it only leads to more appalling questions still." She found that the best plan was to say that she was looking for him, and to "locate him away in the direction in which you wish to travel; this elicits help and sympathy."

Finally she needed a ticket. She noted, with her usual grim humour, that the shipping agents did not issue return tickets on the West African lines of steamers.

She sailed from Liverpool in the beginning of August 1893.

Some years later she said of this departure into the unknown: "Dead tired and feeling no one had need of me any more . . . I went down to West Africa to die. West Africa amused me and was kind to me and was scientifically interesting - and did not want to kill me just then. I am in no hurry. I don't care one way or the other for a year or so."

*   *   *

VOTES FOR WOMEN. APRIL 7, 1911

Dr. Ethel Smyth's Concert.

Dr. Ethel Symth's Concert of Saturday last at the Queen's Hall was not only an important musical event, it was a rallying point for Suffragists eager to show their appreciation of a fellow-worker, and proud of their comrade in the cause.

It was a rousing welcome that Dr. Symth received when she appeared on the platform, and the applause was increased rather than lessened when she announced that, owing to the unexpected defection of Mr. Thomas Beecham, she herself would conduct the entire programme, which she accordingly did, and in right masterly fashion. . .

The concert was brought to an end by the "March of the Women," in which the audience joined with fervour.

THE TIMES, OCTOBER 16 1915

Edith Cavell, 1865 - 1915

Heroic Englishwoman's Sacrifice
Executed By The Germans In Belgium

The Foreign Office are informed by the United States Ambassador that Miss Edith Cavell, lately the head of a large training school for nurses at Brussels, who was arrested on August 5 last by the German authorities at that place, was executed on the 13th inst. after sentence of death had been passed on her.

It is understood that the charge against Miss Cavell was that she had harboured fugitive British and French soldiers and Belgians of military age, and had assisted them to escape from Belgium in order to join the colours.

So far as the Foreign Office are aware, no charge of espionage was brought against her.

THE DAILY TELEGRAPH, APRIL 22 1919

From a Personal Narrative - 1915 - by Brand Whitlock, American Minister to Belgium

Miss Cavell's Last Hours

Our rector, Mr. Gahan, was the last representative of her own people to see Miss Cavell. He had gone from the Legation to the prison of St. Gilles and his wife was among the waiting women on that night at the Legation. Mr. Gahan was with Miss Cavell all that evening . . .

When Mr. Gahan arrived at the prison that night Miss Cavell was lying on the narrow cot in her cell; she arose, drew on a dressing gown, folded it about her thin form and received him calmly . . .

She did not complain of her trial . . . Life had not been all happy for her, she said, and she was glad to die for her country. Life had been hurried, and she was grateful for those weeks of rest in prison.

"Patriotism is not enough" she said; "I must have no hatred and no bitterness toward anyone."

She received the Sacrament, she had no hatred for anyone, and she had no regrets.

Those, as far as we know, were her last words . . . Miss Cavell was brave and calm at the last, and she died facing the firing squad.

THE MANCHESTER GUARDIAN, MAY 15 1919

Edith Cavell

> What dead Queen takes the homage of the Straits
> And enters England by the English gates
> And with a Royal escort? Who is she
> That passes through the land so splendidly?
> An Eleanor, above whose halted bier
> A Cross is set to tell a queen lay here?
> A Mary, borne from Fotheringay to rest
> Where earth is kinder than a sister's breast?
> Nay! 'tis no queen for whom two summer skies
> O'er silent streets of myriad moistened eyes
> In two great capitals a love proclaim
> Scornful of death and innocent of fame;
> No queen - only a simple English nurse
> Slaughtered between a challenge and a curse,
> Who learned her duty where she learned to pray,
> And died as truly as she lives to-day!
> All that she had - and that was life - she gave
> All that she valued - other lives - to save:
> All that we praise, and all we fain would be,
> Is summed in her and her simplicity.
>   J. M. D.

*   *   *

Lilian Baylis, 1874 - 1937

Founder of the National Theatre

After a momentous meeting of the Governors of the Old Vic and Sadler's Wells, Miss Lilian Baylis was asked: "How did you get on?" "Splendidly," she replied; "I had the Almighty in my pocket." She was famous for making odd remarks, which might be meant to be funny and might not; but the import of that statement was deadly in earnest, and both its homeliness and its serene conviction were characteristic of the woman . . .

The best account of Lilian Baylis yet printed is that which Mr. Harcourt Williams has composed, touch by touch, in his book "Four Years at the Old Vic," from which we have borrowed the story in the first sentence. In that book justice is done to her pertinacity in good days and in bad; to the power of her will, which could impose itself upon anyone when she was determined that it should; to the kindness of heart which was not contradicted but expressed by her bracing remarks; and, more than all, to an adroitness, a cleverness, a "slimness" - if we may revive the word for one who had lived in South Africa - by which she got her own way. Ostensibly she knew more about music than about drama; and it is permissible to suppose that, if she had lived to see Sadler's Wells as mature and as popular as the Old Vic, she would have got more personal enjoyment out of its opera and ballet than out of the plays at her other house. But her mission dedicated her to both, and her devotion to the cause won for her a finer judgment in the drama than she cared to admit. When she pretended ignorance it was a ruse to make her people think for themselves, for, having exercised her unerring gift of choice, she would be content with nothing but the very best that they could give her.

In twenty-five years of management she accomplished an incredible work. The Old Vic of her aunt, Miss Cons, was far more a charitable than an artistic enterprise. The Old Vic of Lilian Baylis was not only a permanent repertory theatre for Shakespeare and other drama and an excellent school of acting; it was also the theatre of a new public which it had created for itself, a public ranging through all social degrees and all levels of learning, from erudites on the floor through eager young men and maidens from shops and offices to elementary schoolchildren in the gallery - a people's theatre in the fullest sense.

* * *

ENID HUWS JONES

Margery Fry - The Essential Amateur (1874 - 1958), published 1966

This liveliness of being, fertile in action but undiminished when at rest, had been open to everyone who met her. "We did not even know she was a penal reformer," said one who as a schoolgirl often visited her at Holland Park, "but she seemed to know how to live." Such knowledge, like the development of the delinquent personality, has a lifelong history, and it may be as valuable to preserve the records of the one as of the other.

Margery Fry saw herself always as one of many, though in her later years as one of a group fast disappearing - the single woman of independent means. In this sense, although to others she seemed timeless, she was perfectly clear about her place as an historical figure. She was much else besides, but she was undoubtedly a Victorian spinster, a maiden aunt. She brought to public life an educated judgement, but she also brought the undemanding loving-kindness learnt as a daughter and a sister. On the "surplus women" of her generation and the next, civilization leaned heavily during half a century of violence. Her life was more varied and colourful than most, but the pattern was the same. A few women, like her, became eminent. Few are remembered beyond the annals of one school, one hospital, or one voluntary society. Margery Fry once said that her main work had been to make known the ideas worked out by other people. The work of many spoke through her voice, a voice of great beauty and power. The lives of many may also speak through her life.

105

BARONESS SUMMERSKILL

A Woman's World, 1967

Ruby Mary Webster, 1923 - 1969

This is a woman's book and I will end it by describing two more women's questions on which I have campaigned and on which much still needs to be done. The first was one which I noticed when still a child and it came to a head while I was still in the House of Commons.

Any organization, provided it is sponsored by a Member of Parliament, is permitted to hold a meeting, to which members of the public may be invited, in one of the committee rooms in the House. The competing claims on a Member's time generally mean that a visiting speaker experiences a sense of shock and profound disappointment - which he effectively conceals - on finding only a handful of Members present to listen to his discourse.

Having in my twenty-seven years at Westminster attended many of these gatherings I strolled along the Committee Room corridors one day in November 1965 to a meeting convened by the Rev. Mary Webster, a Congregational Minister, to launch an organization called the "National Council for the Single Woman and her Dependants". It was a miserable day and a thin wet fog spread over the Thames almost obliterating the old buildings of St. Thomas's Hospital opposite. With the bad weather outside the House and the male preponderance inside, I reflected that Miss Webster would be lucky if twenty turned up to the meeting. I felt very sorry for this was the inauguration of the organization. I knew that for three years she had been working hard to persuade the Charity Commissioners to approve the Council; and to organize the single women, who were responsible for the care of elderly parents, to make some protest at the failure of the community to recognize the great contribution which their selfless devotion made to the needs of the elderly and infirm. I was astounded to learn from one of the officials that a room on the Committee Room floor had been reserved for an overflow meeting and that the main gathering was being held in the Grand Committee Room off Westminster Hall, a room big enough to hold eight hundred people if filled to capacity. I

106

lost no time, and on arrival found the Grand Committee Room full, with women standing three deep at the back. Miss Webster, a short, rosy-cheeked, middle-aged woman with twinkling eyes and the unmistakable energy of the good organizer, flanked by a few Members of Parliament among whom I was pleased to see Shirley, gave a brisk, witty, informative address. She said that the problem concerns the last unmarried daughter living at home, caring for elderly and handicapped relatives. Often she has to give up job, friends and pension to stay at home. After years of strain when she is no longer well enough or even qualified to take another job, her dependant dies and she is alone. As I listened my mind went back over the years to a sweet Miss Collins whose life had been devoted to unremitting service to others.

In the 1966 Census a question is included for the first time to find out the number of single women with dependants. The Council will campaign for more equitable tax regulations, for while widows and widowers may claim for a housekeeper, single women may not. It will try to make it easier for single women to get mortgages; it plans to run an advisory service and compile a register of people who could respond to calls in a crisis.

As I looked at this packed gathering of middle aged single women I was struck by the general shabbiness undoubtedly stemming from a life of self-denial; at the sad, unsmiling faces, for a life dedicated to the care of the elderly leaves little room for cheerful social contacts with younger people. When question time came, except for one or two enquiries, the audience remained silent; not because their minds were not crowded with questions which they had asked themselves constantly over the lonely years, but because the silence imposed by habit cannot be easily broken. Aged parents often fail to recognize that a devoted daughter is a grown woman and continue to treat her as a child; their querulous demands on her time and energy must inevitably undermine her will to resist, with the result that she finds in withdrawal her only defence against ceaseless claims on her generosity.

These selfless women are often the butt of cruel music hall jokes; they are called 'old maids' because while women outnumber men, marriage cannot be the lot of everybody ; the presumption is that sexual attraction is the most important criterion by which the human personality should be judged.

107

Many a devoted single daughter is denied a social life which might have enabled her to meet men and subsequently marry and have children of her own. And who could doubt that with her patience and unselfishness she would have made a wonderful mother.

When I came to move the vote of thanks to Mary Webster, I sought to encourage their campaign with a zest and fervour which reminded me of my early campaigning days.

*   *   *

ROSALIND MESSENGER

The Doors of Opportunity, 1967
A Biography of Dame Caroline Haslett 1895 - 1957

"She chafed at the waste of human energy"
In her late teens Caroline had to spend five hours a day on her back in order to strengthen her spine. For some time it seemed doubtful whether she would ever be strong enough to lead a full life. These periods of enforced idleness were of profound importance in her development. As she watched Mother and the other members of the household busy at their daily chores, she chafed at the waste of human energy. Many years later she said in a broadcast:

The kitchen stove burnt coal which had to be brought in buckets from the outhouse, and the flues had to be cleaned and the stove itself polished with blacklead by hand. On washing days the scullery copper was lit and it took all day to get the piles of dirty linen washed. The frilly white underclothes and also the heavily embroidered cotton garments, which were worn at that time, needed heavy starching and ironing, and so the work of the house went on, sweeping, scrubbing, polishing and dusting, all done by hand. No wonder Mother got tired. I did not want to spend my life like that. It seemed a waste of time.

108

She was not prepared meekly to accept the idea that a woman's work is never done. Her reaction was that a limit should be put to a woman's working day, just as it was to a man's, although she had no idea how such improvements could be accomplished. She had heard of electricity during her school lessons, but there is no evidence that she was already dreaming of it as the answer to a woman's prayer. Deep down, she felt it was the system that was at fault. Life should be as interesting and exciting for women as it was for men.

Caroline starts work
'It was a time of very genuine difficulty for me when I left home to live in London, and I wonder how many hundreds, or even thousands of girls were, like myself in 1913, living under great limitations and seeing no chance and no hope for the life for which they vaguely felt themselves fitted.'
So wrote Caroline of the time when she started out to make a career for herself. . .

When the secretarial course was finished, Caroline started work early in 1914 at the London office of the Cochran Boiler Company as a very junior clerk at the handsome wage of ten shillings a week. Her work consisted mainly of drawing up quotations and specifications for the boilers which the company made and sold. She was fortunate in that she worked with men who, after they got over the initial shock of a woman invading their snug masculine preserve, made the work interesting for her. Mr. John Hopkinson of the London office, ironically a strong anti-feminist, succumbed with a charming grace to this feminine invasion, and gave her every encouragement. They became very good friends and he was to play a very important part in her choice of career.
She soon proved her value to the company. By 1918 she was managing the London office, thus relieving a key man for more important work. Managerial responsibility was a challenge to her. It also had its lighter moments. One day she had to visit the War Office about a contract for some boilers. She sent in her card to the officer in charge of contracts and was asked into his office.She entered, the picture of femininity. The officer looked up and a jovial expression crossed his face.
"I expect you have come about typing," the man said, "but I

have to see a fellow about some boilers first. You're a fine looking girl. Come back when he has gone."

Caroline squared her shoulders. There was an amused glint in her clear blue-grey eyes.

"Sir, I am the 'man' who has come about the boilers," she replied sweetly but emphatically.

The officer showed his disbelief. Finally, he accepted that this young girl in front of him was, indeed, Cochran's representative.

"What are we coming to," he jestingly grumbled, "if a wisp of a girl can talk about boilers?"

It was not long, however, before he appreciated that the girl in front of him knew as much about boilers as he did, an awareness that later dawned upon the directors of Caroline's company. They decided she should go to their works in Scotland for practical training in the intricacies of boiler-making, a move that she herself had often requested. . .

SIR HENRY SELF, K.C.B., K.C.M.G., K.B.E., M.SC., PH.D.
(Formerly Chairman, Electricity Council)

A personal appreciation　　　　　　　　　*February 1964*

The British Electricity Authority. . . as a Board comprised four full-time members, four part-time members, and four Area Board chairmen. Caroline Haslett, whilst continuing as Director of the Electrical Association for Women, was one of the four part-time members and she participated in all the Board's fields of responsibility. In addition to first-hand working experience within the industry for a quarter of a century, she had all the essential qualities for undertaking this direct responsibility for its transformation and development; right well did she fulfil her mission! . . .

The Authority functioned largely through standing committees authorized to deal with specific aspects of its responsibilities, whilst shaping the major problems and policies preparatory to final decisions by the Board. Caroline Haslett played an active part in these committees and so came into close touch with the senior officers and staffs of the Authority and the Area Boards. The working relationships which she had established before nationalization now stood her in very good stead and enabled her to associate in all quarters with a certainty of touch and sympathetic insight which worked like a leaven through the whole system. This one woman in the centre became a symbol of good "Human relations", at all levels in a nation-wide organization. She was particularly happy, for example, to represent the Board on the National Joint Advisory Council which had special responsibility for "the safety, health, welfare, education and training, efficiency and other matters of mutual interest of the employees", an appointment which was very much to her liking. She made a great contribution to the establishment of a unique machinery of joint consultation throughout the industry and her colleagues at the centre knew well what her influence meant for the overall *esprit de corps*. . . .

There was yet another wide field of relationships in which she brought great benefit to the industry. Its plan for future growth has been abundantly fulfilled over the past sixteen years, but the provision of vast capital needed and the forward functioning of the expansion schemes have depended largely on its relations with the Government and the ministries, with other public boards, with the trade unions, with private industry, with overseas electricity interests, and with the numerous international agencies for industrial collaboration and mutual sharing of experience. Caroline Haslett rendered a unique service in all these quarters because her extraordinary flair for making effective relationships had been active in all these diverse directions for many years and had made her more than welcome everywhere. The electricity industry in Great Britain had in her a charming advocate and a unique ambassador ; she spent herself in unparalleled devotion to its interests and furthered its aspirations through her wide range of associations outside the industry. ...

She was, indeed, a supreme manifestation of the spirit of humanity at its best.

*　　*　　*

YACHTSWOMAN TELLS WHY SHE SAILED ATLANTIC ALONE.

From Our Correspondent
Southampton, Aug 11

Miss Nicolette Milnes-Walker, aged 28, arrived here today in the Cunard liner Queen Elizabeth 2 after sailing across the Atlantic single-handed in 43 days and predicted that women would enter for the solo transatlantic race next year.

Miss Milnes-Walker, a research psychologist of the University of Wales Institute of Science and Technology, Cardiff, left Dale, Pembrokeshire, on June 12 in her 30ft sloop Aziz, and arrived at Newport, Rhode Island, on July 26.

She said today that she went on the trip to see how she would react. "I think it has taught me the difference between important things and trivial things. I have become more impulsive about things that don't really matter but take more trouble over important things."

The journey had been a rewarding experience. It had been a satisfying experience to be alone on the sea.

She had been in fear of her life at times. "But I think that it was irrational because I don't think my life was in danger" she said.

"Sometimes I wore a shirt and bikini pants, but much of the time wore nothing at all. When I was on deck it was a choice between putting on oilskins and becoming waterproof or taking everything off and being waterproof. I took everything off.

"The worst moment was when two whales circled the tiny yacht. They were about 50 to 60ft long, and played like dolphins", she said.

She had to ride out a bad storm about 500 miles off the American coast and drifted without sails for two days.

Much of her free time on her voyage was spent reading books, including Shakespeare's *The Tempest*. She also sang hymns and made notes for a book she is writing.

She hopes to finish the book in a few weeks. It will be called *When I Put Out to Sea.*

NICOLETTE MILNES-WALKER

When I Put Out to Sea, 1972

It is an odd feeling, being a celebrity. How easy it would be to believe what is said about one. But often I hardly recognise myself in the glowing descriptions and am careful to remain myself and not become the fictional public figure. I am still the woman who, less than a year ago, conceived the idea of a solo Atlantic crossing. Of course I have changed in some ways. I am more confident of myself, and therefore more able to be open and honest with myself and others. My experience of the Atlantic and the subsequent events has made me more receptive to new ideas and new experiences and my pleasure in life has been enhanced. But I remain myself, Nicolette, a twenty-eight year old, five foot four inch, eight stone woman. I would not wish to be anyone else.

Neither would I do the same trip again, for one cannot repeat a new experience. I don't think I would do anything alone for a long period, not because I dislike being alone but because when you share an experience with someone the experience is enhanced, both as it happens and in retrospect. I look forward to new journeys of discovery. Of discovering myself. Writing this book has been one. I am going to make sure that there are others. Now my mind has come alive I am not going to let it die.

11

THE POLITICIANS

HANSARD, 3rd AUGUST, 1832

Prayer of petition presented by Mr. Hunt M.P. on behalf of Mary Smith, of Stanmore in the county of York.

"Every unmarried female possessing the necessary pecuniary qualification should be entitled to vote for Members of Parliament."

*   *   *

JOHN STUART MILL, 1806 - 1873

The Subjection of Women, 1869

There is nothing, after disease, indigence, and guilt, so fatal to the pleasureable enjoyment of life as the want of a worthy outlet for the active faculties. Women who have the cares of a family, and while they have the cares of a family, have this outlet, and it generally suffices for them: but what of the greatly increasing number of women, who have had no opportunity of exercising the vocation which they are mocked by telling them is their proper one? What of the women whose children have been lost to them by death or distance, or have grown up, married, and formed homes of their own? There are abundant examples of men who, after a life engrossed by business, retire with a competency to the enjoyment, as they hope, of rest, but to whom, as they are unable to acquire new interests and excitements that can replace the old, the change to a life of inactivity brings ennui, melancholy, and premature death. Yet no one thinks of the parallel case of so many worthy and devoted women, who, having paid what they are told is their debt to society - having brought up a family blamelessly to manhood and womanhood - having kept a house as long as they had a house needing to be kept - are deserted by the sole occupation for which they have fitted themselves; and remain with undiminished activity but with no employment for it, unless perhaps a daughter or daughter-in-law is willing to abdicate in their favour the discharge of the same functions in her younger household. Surely a hard lot for the old age of those who have worthily discharged, as long as it was given to them to discharge, what the world accounts their only social duty. Of such women, and of those others to whom this duty has not been committed at all - many of whom pine through life with the consciousness of thwarted vocations, and activities which are not suffered to expand - the only resources, speaking generally, are religion and charity. But their religion, though it may be one of feeling, and of ceremonial observance, cannot be a religion of action, unless in the form of charity. For charity many of them are by nature admirably fitted; but to practise it usefully, or even without doing mischief, requires the education, the manifold preparation, the knowledge and the thinking powers, of a skilful administrator. There are few of the administrative functions of government for which a person would not be fit, who is fit to bestow charity usefully. In this as in other cases (pre-eminently in that of the education of children), the duties permitted to women cannot be performed properly, without their being trained for duties which, to the great loss of society, are not permitted to them.

*   *   *

CHRISTABEL PANKHURST, 1880 - 1958

Unshackled: The Story of how we won the Vote, 1959

Militancy really began on 20th February 1904, at a first Free Trade Hall meeting with a protest of which little was heard and nothing remembered - because it did not result in imprisonment!

The Free Trade League, a renaissance of the Anti-Corn Law organization, had announced its initial meeting in the Free Trade Hall to be addressed by Mr. Winston Churchill. I applied for a ticket and received one for the platform. This was excellent for my purpose. Mr. Churchill had moved that 'this meeting affirms its unshakable belief in the principles of Free Trade adopted more than fifty years ago . . .'; others had seconded and supported the resolution, when, as related by the *Manchester Guardian:*

> Miss Pankhurst asked to be allowed to move an amendment with regard to Woman Suffrage. The Chairman said he was afraid he could not permit such an addition. It contained words and sentiments on a matter more or less contentious to which persons absolutely agreed on the question of Free Trade might have difficulty in giving their support. Miss Pankhurst seemed loth to give way, but finally, amid loud cries of 'Chair', she retired. The Chairman read the addition which Miss Pankhurst proposed to make to the resolution which asked that the Representation of the People Acts should be so amended that the words importing the masculine gender should include women. He was sorry, he said that he must adhere to his decision not to put it.

This was the first militant step - the hardest to me, because it *was* the first. To move from my place on the platform to the speaker's table in the teeth of the astonishment and opposition of will of that immense throng, those civic and county leaders and those Members of Parliament, was the most difficult thing I have ever done.

Something had been gained. Women's claim to vote had been imposed upon the attention of political leaders and the public, at one of the decisive political meetings of the century. The trouble was that the thought of woman suffrage quickly faded. I reproached myself for having given way too easily. Next time such a meeting was held, a mark should be made that could not disappear. Thus militancy had its origin in purpose.

THE RT. HON. FREDERICK WILLIAM
BARON PETHICK-LAWRENCE

Address at the Memorial Service for Dame Christabel Pankhurst DBE., at St. Martin-in-the-Fields, March 14th, 1958.

Dear Friends,
We are met together here to-day to commemorate a woman whose great life work in this country was performed half a century ago. Christabel Pankhurst was in 1905 a young woman of great charm and beauty. She had a keen feminine intuition and a brain which had already won her university distinction and was to prove a match for some of the best brains of the day. Possessed of such gifts, a woman even fifty years ago could be assured of an easy road to self fulfilment and personal pre-eminence. But Christabel brushed aside this opportunity and chose instead to fight for the emancipation of her sex from its age-long subjection.
People living to-day, when the equality of men and women is - at least conventionally - accepted, find it difficult to look back to the beginning of the century when this idea was commonly regarded as palpably untrue. It was not merely that most men were unwilling to concede equal citizenship to women; it was also the fact that women themselves were apathetic and disinclined to make any effort to improve their status. It was left to a small band of stalwarts of both sexes to plead the cause.
It was therefore a formidable task that Christabel undertook when she set out to rouse women to a sense of their own worth and dignity and to make use of this new-found resolution to break down the walls of prejudice and opposition. She herself adopted shock tactics. She interrupted a political meeting, created a symbolic obstruction in a public street and underwent the indignity of a prison sentence as a common miscreant.

117

The result was very much what might have been anticipated. The world lifted an eyebrow and smiled derisorily. How absurd it was to imagine that this silly and rather disreputable escapade would promote the cause of women. Of course it could only have the opposite effect. It would show how unfit women were to be trusted with equal citizenship.

But Christabel thought otherwise. And we, looking back over the fifty years of intervening history, are forced to the conclusion that the world's forecast of the future was wrong and that of the young girl was right.

This is not the time or the place to tell in detail the story of the struggle that ensued. Suffice it to say that great numbers of people from all walks of life enlisted under the standard of revolt that Christabel raised. Among them were persons of note of both sexes. Doctors, authors, actors, university graduates, nurses, teachers accepted her leadership and carried out her bidding. For several years the contest raged with varying fortunes. When the war clouds broke in 1914 Votes for Women had become one of the foremost political issues of the day.

Christabel then decided (there is no doubt rightly) that when the life of the nation was at stake there could be no internecine divisions at home. Women offered their services to the Government in many capacities and their offers were after some hesitation accepted. Their contribution proved invaluable. Before peace was made in Europe peace with victory was secured by the women of our own country.

Of Christabel's later years spent in a foreign land and devoted to a different cause I am not competent to speak. But those who shared her life in California have written to tell me of her continuing charm, of the power and eloquence of her address and of the spell which she exerted over the circle of friends in which they moved.

There are few people of whom it can be said that they changed the course of human history and that they changed it for the better. But this can with confidence be said of Christabel Pankhurst.

Therefore let us to-day praise this famous woman. May her memory inspire us to lives of high and noble endeavour for the upliftment of mankind.

JOSEPHINE KAMM

Rapiers and Battleaxes, 1966

Susan Lawrence, 1871 - 1947

Susan Lawrence . . . daughter of a solicitor, . . . was awarded an exhibition for pure mathematics at University College, London, and finished her education at Newnham College, Cambridge. She started out as a Conservative, and as such was co-opted to the education committee of the London County Council and was elected as a Municipal Reform candidate in 1910. To Socialists this dashing looking, slim young woman, who wore a monocle and drove round Hyde Park in a dog-cart, was a reactionary of the deepest dye. Her conversion to Socialism which occurred in 1912 was as sudden as it was complete. She had taken part with Mary Macarthur in an enquiry into the conditions of women cleaners ; and was so horrified by what she learned that she switched from Right to Left almost overnight, to become the most sincere and hard working of social reformers. . . .

Susan Lawrence had plenty of courage. She took great pains to make her voice acceptable (she had already put away her monocle and her dog-cart) : and she won excellent opinions for her work for the Women's Trade Union League.
In 1913, as member for Poplar, Susan Lawrence was the first Labour woman member of the LCC. Some years later she and her Poplar colleagues were sent to prison for refusing to collect the Poor Rate, which they considered far too heavy for the borough to carry alone. Margaret Bondfield, who visited her in Holloway, found her out in the corridor smoking a cigarette, and was told that the whole affair was nothing but a great lark. But the Poplar member's protest bore fruit ; for the burden of Poor Law relief became more centralized.
Susan Lawrence first held Government office in 1924 as Parliamentary Private Secretary to the President of the Board of Education; and in 1929, in the second Labour Government, she was Parliamentary Secretary to the Ministry of Health. She lost her seat in the General Election which followed the financial crisis of 1931 and did not stand again. She had, however, become a byword for the clarity and caustic

humour of her speeches ; she was the only woman MP of her day who never missed a division or an all-night sitting ; and she made a small piece of history when she defied the Speaker's ruling by refusing to cover her close-cropped grey head when she raised a point of order.

*　*　*

BARONESS STOCKS

Eleanor Rathbone, 1949

Eleanor Rathbone, 1872 - 1946

Eleanor Rathbone was not, of course, the first of her line to emerge as a notable public figure. Five generations of Rathbones had been public figures. In the history of the city of Liverpool no sooner does one Rathbone pass from the scene after a chronicle of ardent warfare against oppression, corruption, apathy, destitution or ignorance, as the case may be, than another Rathbone steps forward to open a new chapter of energetic reforming zeal. . . .

The First World War brought Eleanor into the forefront of civic politics in her own right as a "Rathbone regnant" - the seventh of her dynasty, to accept without reservation those "unsuspected obligations" of Liverpool citizenship. . . .

Eleanor's public responsibilities multiplied. She had achieved the stage at which, in her own city, she was the obvious incumbent of any administrative office which had reached the point of accepting the services of a woman; and many of her new responsibilities were of her own making. . . .

Family allowances became her major, though by no means her only preoccupation in the years which followed the war.

120

DIANA HOPKINSON

The Incense - Tree, 1968

We stayed one holiday at the Red House near Keswick with
Eleanor Rathbone. That stalwart warrior of women's rights
remained ensconced in her drawing-room dressed in her
London black, impressive pearls about her neck, surrounded
by Blue Books and puffing Turkish cigarettes. A child who
asked her a question had to wait for the answer while the
distant look in Eleanor's eyes faded as she returned from
consideration of some political problem. Then she smiled
majestically - almost jovially - and gave a full and gentle
answer. She once told my mother - possibly in a moment of
weakness - that she would have gladly exchanged her entire
political career for marriage and children.

*　　*　　*

JOSEPHINE KAMM

Rapiers and Battleaxes, 1966

Margaret Bondfield, 1873 - 1953

Margaret Bondfield . . . the first woman Cabinet Minister, had
fought her way up from almost impossibly difficult beginnings. This eager, intelligent woman was the tenth child of
a Somerset lace-maker, and although her parents did not
know grinding poverty it was no easy task for them to bring up
a family of eleven. At the age of eleven, Margaret Bondfield started work as an assistant in a Brighton draper's
shop. Wages were deplorably low: living-in conditions were
drab and sordid. The women slept in a bleak, bare dormitory;
they had no privacy, and nowhere to keep their belongings
except in a box under the bed. It was most fortunate that the
girl who in later life did so much to improve the pay and
conditions of shopworkers should have met at this juncture a
middle-aged widow whose concern for the underprivileged
had led her to keep open house for Brighton shop assistants.

She was Mrs. Louisa Martindale, mother of two daughters one of whom became a doctor, the other a high ranking Civil Servant. Louisa Martindale, as Margaret Bondfield wrote after her death, 'had the gift of drawing out the best from others:' and she herself never forgot the sympathetic help she had received.

At the age of twenty, with £5 in her pocket, Margaret Bondfield went to London. After three frightening months of unemployment she found a living-in job in a shop where she had to work a 65-hour week for an annual wage of £15, rising by stages to £25. Chancing to see a letter in a newspaper from the Secretary of the Shop Assistants' Union urging employees to combine in an effort to secure better conditions, she hurried round to the Union's headquarters. From that time onwards she spent all her free time on Union work; and when in 1896 she was invited by the Women's Industrial Council to undertake an enquiry into shop conditions, she accepted, realizing that never again would she be allowed to work in a shop. The enquiry, which lasted two years, formed the basis of evidence which was later submitted to the Royal Commission on Shop Workers. In 1898 Margaret Bondfield was appointed Assistant Secretary of the Union, and devoted several years to campaigning for shorter hours and better pay and conditions; and in 1899, as the only woman delegate to the Trades Union Congress, she spoke in support of the resolution which led to the creation of the Labour Party. She was also on the committee of the Women's Trade Union League which had developed from Emma Paterson's Women's Protective and Provident League; and she worked under the women's labour organizer Mary Macarthur (1880 - 1921) who in 1906 welded the local unions of women workers into the National Federation of Women Workers. By 1923, when Margaret Bondfield was elected to Parliament, considerable improvements had been made in shop and factory conditions. In 1923 she was elected Chairman of the Trades Union Congress; but her appointment to the Government as Parliamentary Secretary to the Ministry of Labour prevented her from presiding over the 1924 conference. She lost her seat at the General Election the same year but was re-elected in 1926. But with the fall of the Labour Government in 1931 'the Right Honourable Margaret' left politics and returned to Trades Union work, representing the Government or the workers on a number of missions overseas. In 1948 she was made Companion of Honour, a tribute to her ability and achievements, her integrity and downright common sense.

*　　*　　*

JOSEPHINE KAMM

Rapiers and Battleaxes, 1966

Ellen Wilkinson, 1891 - 1947

Known as 'Red Ellen', for her flaming red hair as much as for her politics, Ellen Wilkinson was the third of the four children of a Manchester cotton operative; and she passed by way of scholarships from elementary to secondary school and thence to Manchester University. When she came down from the University Ellen Wilkinson became a pupil-teacher, but her inclination was towards journalism for which she had a very decided gift. In 1913 she became an organizer of the National Union of Women's Suffrage Societies, although the aggressiveness and emotional force of her later speeches seem to suggest that she might have been more at home among the militants. In the same year she was made National Organizer of the National Union of Distributive and Allied Workers. In 1924 her flirtation with Communism came to an end; she severed her ties with the Party and was elected to Parliament as Socialist Member for Middlesbrough East; and for the rest of her life she fought Communism within her Trade Union. After serving as Parliamentary Private Secretary to Susan Lawrence at the Ministry of Health, Ellen Wilkinson lost her seat in the 1931 debacle; but in 1935 she was elected Socialist Member for Jarrow and held this seat until her death. It was fitting that this loyal and vital woman who could seldom resist a fight should represent Jarrow at the time of the slump. In and out of Parliament she laboured for the depressed areas of the north-east; and in 1936 she led the unemployed Jarrow marchers to London, walking most of the way herself, and cheering the 2,000 men who marched behind her. 'Come on, let's have a song,' cried Miss Perky, as she was often called.

'We may be wet but we don't have to look it.' Three years later in her most important book, *The Town that was Murdered,* Ellen Wilkinson gave a detailed history of the shipyard closure and its disastrous consequences.

Inside Parliament Ellen Wilkinson scored a notable success in 1935 when she introduced a Private Members' Bill designed to stop certain flagrant abuses of the hire purchase system and carried it through with support from three Parties. She was a member of Winston Churchill's Coalition Government, first as Parliamentary Secretary to the Ministry of Pensions and then as Parliamentary Secretary to the Ministry of Home Security. She took her responsibilities for Civil Defence very seriously, and the lack of adequate air-raid precautions in London and the other large cities galvanized her into a tremendous burst of activity. She drove her own car through the blitz to spend her nights in uncomfortable air-raid shelters and did much to counteract Communist efforts to spread disaffection. She survived two narrow escapes from bombs; but the energy she expended after a long day's work and the nervous tension engendered by her shelter activities seriously affected her health; it had never been good, and all her life she had to battle with asthma and bronchitis.

In 1945 Ellen Wilkinson became the second woman to reach Cabinet rank, as Minister of Education in Mr. (now Lord) Attlee's Labour Government. She had already been concerned with the changes made in the structure of education by the Education Act of 1944; now she had the task of carrying on from Mr. R. A. (now Lord) Butler. It was tragic that she should have died at the age of fifty-five, just when her loyalty to people and causes and her fighting instincts might have been canalized into real statesmanship.

* * *

124

12

VICTORIANA

GERTRUDE BELL

The other day I did so want you to be here so that you might see Miss Wordsworth's best cap. To the uninitiated eye it looks like a bundle of flowers tied together by a ribbon of velvet and then a row of lace all round. It's very very little (and you know Miss Wordsworth's head is very wide and large) and generally it's crooked! All her best caps are as little as that, but they are not all quite so fine! . . .

*   *   *

CHARLES DICKENS, 1812 - 1870

The Life and Adventures of Nicholas Nickleby, 1838

Filial Self-Sacrifice

"My nephew, Frank, I say," resumed Mr. Cheeryble, "encountered her by accident, and lost sight of her almost in a minute afterwards, within two days after he returned to England. Her father lay in some secret place to avoid his creditors, reduced, between sickness and poverty, to the verge of death, and she, a child - we might almost think, if we did not know the wisdom of all Heaven's decrees - who should have blessed a better man, was steadily braving privation, degradation, and everything most terrible to such a young and delicate creature's heart, for the purpose of supporting him. She was attended, sir," said brother Charles, "in these reverses, by one faithful creature, who had been, in old times,

125

a poor kitchen wench in the family, who was then their solitary servant, but who might have been for the truth and fidelity of her heart - who might have been - ah! the wife of Tim Linkinwater himself, sir!"

Pursuing this encomium upon the poor follower with such energy and relish as no words can describe, brother Charles leant back in his chair, and delivered the remainder of his relation with greater composure.

It was in substance this: That proudly resisting all offers of permanent aid and support from her late mother's friends, because they were made conditional upon her quitting the wretched man, her father, who had no friends left, and shrinking with instinctive delicacy from appealing in their behalf to that true and noble heart which he hated, and had, through its greatest and purest goodness, deeply wronged by misconstruction and ill report, this young girl had struggled alone and unassisted to maintain him by the labour of her hands. That through the utmost depths of poverty and affliction she had toiled, never turning aside for an instant from her task, never wearied by the petulant gloom of a sick man sustained by no consoling recollections of the past or hopes of the future; never repining for the comforts she had rejected, or bewailing the hard lot she had voluntarily incurred. That every little accomplishment she had acquired in happier days had been put into requisition for this purpose, and directed to this one end. That for two long years, toiling by day and often too by night, working at the needle, the pencil, and the pen, and submitting, as a daily governess, to such caprices and indignities as women (with daughters too) too often love to inflict upon their sex when they serve in such capacities, as though in jealousy of the superior intelligence which they are necessitated to employ - indignities, in ninety-nine cases out of every hundred, heaped upon persons immeasurably and incalculably their betters, but outweighing in comparison any that the most heartless blackleg would put upon his groom - that for two long years, by dint of labouring in all these capacities and wearying in none, she had not succeeded in the sole aim and object of her life, but that, overwhelmed by accumulated difficulties and disappointments, she had been compelled to seek out her mother's old friend, and, with a bursting heart, to confide in him at last.

"If I had been poor," said brother Charles, with sparkling

126

eyes; "if I had been poor, Mr. Nickleby, my dear sir, which of course thank God I am not, I would have denied myself (of course anybody would under such circumstances) the commonest necessaries of life to help her. As it is, the task is a difficult one. If her father were dead, nothing could be easier, for then she should share and cheer the happiest home that brother Ned and I could have, as if she were our child or sister. But he is still alive. Nobody can help him; that has been tried a thousand times; he was not abandoned by all without good cause, I know."

*　　*　　*

MRS. SARAH STICKNEY ELLIS, 1810 - 1872

The Women of England, 1839

When we meet in society with that speechless, inanimate ignorant, and useless being called "a young lady just come from school," it is thought a sufficient apology for all her deficiencies, that she has, poor thing! but just come home from school. Thus implying that nothing in the way of domestic usefulness, social intercourse, or adaptation to circumstances, can be expected from her until she has had time to learn it.

If, during the four or five years spent at school, she had been establishing herself upon the foundation of her future character, and learning to practise what would afterwards be the business of her life, she would, when her education was considered as complete, be in the highest possible state of perfection which her nature, at that season of life, would admit of. This is what she ought to be. I need not advert to what she is.

I still cling fondly to the hope, that ere long, some system of female instruction will be discovered, by which the young women of England may be sent home from school prepared for the stations appointed them by Providence to fill in after life, and prepared to fill them well. Then indeed may this favoured country boast of her privileges, when her young women return to their homes and their parents, habituated to be on the watch for every opportunity of doing good to others; making it the first and the last inquiry of every day, "What can I do to make my parents, my brothers, or my sisters, more happy? I am but a feeble instrument in the hands of Providence, to work out any of his benevolent designs; but as he will give me strength, I hope to pursue the plan to which I have become accustomed, of seeking my own happiness only in the happiness of others."

*　　*　　*

ELIZABETH S. HALDANE, 1862 - 1937

From One Century to Another, 1937

"The most splendid of nurses"
My earliest memories are of a big nursery in a beautiful Edinburgh square. . . it was lit by two unshaded gas lights, one over the table in the middle of the room, the other, only lighted if necessary, at the fireplace. At the fire on a low nursing chair sat the most splendid of nurses reading the news, spectacles on eyes and with a black velvet and lace cap on head: a silk apron protected her full skirt. She was probably reading the report of the Tichborne case - a case that gave reading for months - giving utterance to her thoughts about it from time to time; or else she was exploring the new Education Bill and expressing fears, despite her deep value for education, that no longer would young servants be found. With that she would carry her eyes to the under-nurse who seemed to be living a blameless life carrying hot water and dinners up three or four flights of stairs, always carefully avoiding the gentry in so doing, and otherwise behaving as young servants should. That is to say they must wear cotton 'prints' in the morning which cost 7s 11d. to make up and were bought out of their £12 of wages; black dresses and black

bonnets in the afternoon. No hats nor feathers. How they paid for dress, shoes and everything I cannot think, but they did, and saved for their parents. Our nurse had £25 a year, and each half-year (for wages were paid half-yearly in those days) she made a solemn expedition to the savings bank and another to the post office in order to put money in the bank and send home a money order. Nurses, once they had embarked on their career, had to make up their minds to see no more of their relatives, for holidays there were none. Our nurse always carried the babies in her own arms; she would have disdained a perambulator or any mechanical aid. In my wildest fancy I could not imagine my mother bathing or dressing me, and she never thought of such a thing. To my mind she was always as she appeared in the nursery near bedtime, a lovely figure in a beautiful moiré silk gown so widely spread out that when the boys' tutor came into the room unexpectedly she simply floated her frock over bath and child together, forming for the latter a delightful tent.

*　　*　　*

BARBARA STEPHEN, 1872 -1945

Emily Davies and Girton College, 1927

"Daughters should have an equal provision with sons"
Mr. Leigh Smith held the unusual opinion that daughters should have an equal provision with sons. He did not adopt the ordinary plan of paying his daughters' bills and giving them an occasional present, but when Barbara * came of age in 1848 he gave her an allowance of £300 a year. Money was to her, as she wrote in one of her pamphlets, "a power to do good . . . a responsibility which we must accept." We can gather how she liked to spend hers; "if you get money," she

---

* Barbara Leigh Smith - later Mrs. Bodichon, benefactor of Girton College.

writes, "you gain a power of sending a child to school, of buying a good book to give to the ignorant, of sending a sick person to a good climate, etc." Generosity was the keynote of her character, and she enjoyed the hospitality which she had the power of exercising. At Scalands, near Robertsbridge, she built a small house of red brick, in the style of an old Sussex cottage - probably one of the earliest attempts to introduce a more beautiful kind of domestic architecture in place of the devastating ugliness which held sway before the time of William Morris. Among her early visitors here were D.G. Rossetti and Miss Siddal, in 1854, when the "indefatigable and invaluable Barbara," as Rossetti calls her, was trying to help them with plans for the benefit of Miss Siddal's health. Freedom and responsibility, and the sympathy of her elders, encouraged Barbara's natural feeling of public spirit, and enabled her to do things which were then unusual and unconventional with a remarkable absence of self-consciousness. As a friend wrote of her, she was "grandly innocent and simple." She had none of the painful struggles and conscientious scruples and conventions which made it hard for other women (such as her cousin Florence Nightingale, who was brought up in a much more conventional home) to follow their bent. Another cousin, Mrs. Albert Dicey, in recalling a long visit which first made her well acquainted with Barbara, describes her aptly: "I had till that year never come across any woman who was so much of a *citizen.*"

VIRGINIA WOOLF, 1882 - 1941

Three Guineas, 1938

"He appealed to her womanhood"
There is the case of Mr. Jex-Blake. Here we have the case of a father who is not confronted with his daughter's marriage but with his daughter's wish to earn her living. That wish also would seem to have aroused in the father a very strong

emotion and an emotion which also seems to have its origin in the levels below conscious thought. Again with your leave we will call it a case of infantile fixation. The daughter, Sophia, was offered a small sum for teaching mathematics; and she asked her father's permission to take it. That permission was instantly and heatedly refused. "Dearest, I have only this moment heard that you contemplate being *paid* for the tutorship. It would be quite beneath you, darling, and I *cannot consent* to it." (The italics are the father's.) "Take the post as one of honour and usefulness, and I shall be glad. . . . But to be *paid* for the work would be to alter the thing *completely*, and would lower you sadly in the eyes of almost everybody." That is a very interesting statement. Sophia, indeed, was led to argue the matter. Why was it beneath her, she asked, why should it lower her? Taking money for work did not lower Tom in anybody's eyes. That, Mr. Jex-Blake explained, was quite a different matter; Tom was a man; Tom "feels bound as a *man* . . . to support his wife and family"; Tom had therefore taken "the *plain path* of duty." Still Sophia was not satisfied. She argued - not only was she poor and wanted the money; but also she felt strongly "the honest, and I believe perfectly justifiable pride of earning." Thus pressed Mr. Jex-Blake at last gave, under a semi-transparent cover, the real reason why he objected to her taking money. He offered to give her the money himself if she would refuse to take it from the College. It was plain, therefore, that he did not object to her taking money; what he objected to was her taking money from another man. The curious nature of his proposal did not escape Sophia's scrutiny. "In that case," she said, "I must say to the Dean, not, 'I am willing to work without payment,' but 'My Father prefers that I should receive payment from *him*, not from the College,' and I think the Dean would think us both ridiculous, or at least foolish." Whatever interpretation the Dean might have put upon Mr. Jex-Blake's behaviour, we can have no doubt what emotion was at the root of it. He wished to keep his daughter in his own power. If she took money from him she remained in his power; if she took it from another man not only was she becoming independent of Mr. Jex-Blake, she was becoming dependent upon another man. That he wished her to depend upon him, and felt obscurely that this desirable dependence could only be secured by financial dependence is proved indirectly by

131

another of his veiled statements. "If you married to-morrow to my liking - and I don't believe you would ever marry otherwise - I should give you a good fortune." If she became a wage-earner, she could dispense with the fortune and marry whom she liked. The case of Mr. Jex-Blake is very easily diagnosed, but it is a very important case because it is a normal case, a typical case. Mr. Jex-Blake was no monster of Wimpole Street; he was an ordinary father; he was doing what thousands of other Victorian fathers whose cases remain unpublished were doing daily. It is a case, therefore, that explains much that lies at the root of Victorian psychology - that psychology of the sexes which is still, Professor Grensted tells us, so obscure. The case of Mr. Jex-Blake shows that the daughter must not on any account be allowed to make money because if she makes money she will be independent of her father and free to marry any man she chooses. Therefore the daughter's desire to earn her living rouses two different forms of jealousy. Each is strong separately; together they are very strong. It is further significant that in order to justify this very strong emotion which has its origin below the levels of conscious thought Mr. Jex-Blake had recourse to one of the commonest of all evasions; the argument which is not an argument but an appeal to the emotions. He appealed to the very deep, ancient and complex emotion which we may, as amateurs, call the womanhood emotion. To take money was beneath her he said; if she took money she would lower herself in the eyes of almost everybody. Tom being a man would not be lowered; it was her sex that made the difference. He appealed to her womanhood.

Whenever a man makes that appeal to a woman he rouses in her, it is safe to say, a conflict of emotions of a very deep and primitive kind which it is extremely difficult for her to analyse or reconcile . . . Her first instinct was to attack the most obvious form of womanhood, that which lay uppermost in her consciousness and seemed to be responsible for her father's attitude - her ladyhood. Like other educated men's daughters, Sophia Jex-Blake was what is called 'a lady' . . . "Do you honestly, father, think" she asked, "any lady lowered by the mere act of receiving money?"

*   *   *

132

MRS. ELIZABETH CLEGHORN GASKELL, 1810 - 1865

Cranford, 1853

"Don't be frightened by Miss Pole from getting married"
Miss Pole began a long congratulation to Miss Matty that so
far they had escaped marriage, which she noticed always made
people credulous to the last degree; indeed, she thought it
argued great natural credulity in a woman if she could not
keep herself from being married; and in what Lady Glenmire
had said about Mr. Hoggins' robbery we had a specimen of
what people came to if they gave way to such a weakness;
evidently Lady Glenmire would swallow anything if she could
believe the poor vamped-up story about a neck of mutton and
a pussy with which he had tried to impose on Miss Pole, only
she had always been on her guard against believing too much
of what men said.
We were thankful, as Miss Pole desired us to be, that we had
never been married; but I think, of the two, we were even more
thankful that the robbers had left Cranford; at least I judge so
from a speech of Miss Matty's that evening, as we sat over the
fire, in which she evidently looked upon a husband as a great
protector against thieves, burglars, and ghosts; and said, that
she did not think that she should dare to be always warning
young people against matrimony, as Miss Pole did
continually; - to be sure, marriage was a risk, as she saw now
she had had some experience; but she remembered the time
when she had looked forward to being married as much as any
one.
"Not to any particular person, my dear," said she, hastily
checking herself up as if she were afraid of having admitted
too much; "only the old story, you know, of ladies always
saying *"When* I marry," and gentlemen, *"If* I marry." It was a
joke spoken in rather a sad tone, and I doubt if either of us
smiled; but I could not see Miss Matty's face by the flickering
fire-light. In a little while she continued:
"But after all I have not told you the truth. It is so long ago,
and no one ever knew how much I thought of it at the time,
unless, indeed, my dear mother guessed; but I may say that
there was a time when I did not think I should have been only

Miss Matty Jenkyns all my life; for even if I did meet with any one who wished to marry me now (and as Miss Pole says, one is never too safe), I could not take him - I hope he would not take it too much to heart, but I could *not* take him - or any one but the person I once thought I should be married to, and he is dead and gone, and he never knew how it all came about that I said 'No,' when I had thought many and many a time—— Well, it's no matter what I thought. God ordains it all, and I am very happy, my dear. No one has such kind friends as I," continued she, taking my hand and holding it in hers.

If I had never known of Mr. Holbrook, I could have said something in this pause, but as I had, I could not think of anything that would come in naturally, and so we both kept silence for a little time.

"My father once made us," she began, "keep a diary, in two columns; on one side we were to put down in the morning what we thought would be the course and events of the coming day, and at night we were to put down on the other side what really had happened, It would be to some people rather a sad way of telling their lives" - (a tear dropped upon my hand at these words) - "I don't mean that mine has been sad, only so very different to what I expected. I remember, one winter's evening, sitting over our bedroom fire with Deborah - I remember it as if it were yesterday - and we were planning our future lives - both of us were planning, though only she talked about it. She said she should like to marry an archdeacon, and write his charges; and you know, my dear, she never was married, and, for aught I know, she never spoke to an unmarried archdeacon in her life. I never was ambitious, nor could I have written charges, but I thought I could manage a house (my mother used to call me her right hand), and I was always so fond of little children - the shyest babies would stretch out their little arms to come to me; when I was a girl, I was half my leisure time nursing in the neighbouring cottages - but I don't know how it was , when I grew sad and grave - which I did a year or two after this time - the little things drew back from me, and I am afraid I lost the knack, though I am just as fond of children as ever, and have a strange yearning at my heart whenever I see a mother with her baby in her arms. Nay, my dear" - (and by a sudden blaze which sprang up from a fall of the unstirred coals, I saw that her eyes were full of

134

tears - gazing intently on some vision of what might have been) - "do you know, I dream sometimes that I have a little child - always the same - a little girl of about two years old; she never grows older, though I have dreamt about her for many years. I don't think I ever dream of any words or sound she makes; she is very noiseless and still, but she comes to me when she is very sorry or very glad, and I have wakened with the clasp of her dear little arms round my neck. Only last night - perhaps because I had gone to sleep thinking of this ball for Phoebe - my little darling came in my dream, and put up her mouth to be kissed, just as I have seen real babies do to real mothers before going to bed. But all this is nonsense, dear! only don't be frightened by Miss Pole from being married. I can fancy it may be a very happy state, and a little credulity helps one on through life very smoothly, - better than always doubting and doubting, and seeing difficulties and disagreeables in everything."

* * *

ANONYMOUS

From a Family Album, 1826 - 1869

Old Maids
A sprightly writer expressed his opinion of Old Maids in the following manner: I am inclined to believe that many of the satirical aspersions cast upon Old Maids tell more to their credit than is generally imagined. Is a woman remarkably neat in her person "She will assuredly die an Old Maid". Is she particularly reserved towards the other sex "She has all the squeamishness of an Old Maid". Is she frugal in her expenses, and exact in her domestic concerns "She is cut out for an Old Maid". And if she is kindly humane to the animals about her, nothing can save her from the appellation of an "Old Maid". In short, I have always found that neatness, modesty, economy and humanity are the never-failing characteristics of that terrible creature - "an Old Maid".

135

VERA WHEATLEY

The Life and Work of Harriet Martineau, 1957

Harriet Martineau, 1802 - 1876

"Old enough - at fifty two - to be addressed as 'Mrs' "
A few years before this, she had written to Mrs. Weston
Chapman to say that she thought she was now old enough - at
fifty-two - to be addressed as "Mrs". "Wasn't there Mrs.
Hannah More & Mrs. Edgeworth? . . . I will be Mrs. Harriet
Martineau." In a letter to Philip Carpenter, with whom she
sustained a lively correspondence for many years, she asks him
henceforward to address her as "Mrs." "Joanna Baillie,
Hannah More & Elizabeth Carter were all under 52 when they
laid down the Miss." But on the whole, her friends and the
public at large were true to their first affection and would
never call her anything but "Miss Martineau".

*   *   *

MRS. A. J. PENNY

The Afternoon of Unmarried Life, 1858

To
*The Unmarried Gentlewomen of England
Whom Time has made Familiar with Sorrow
And not Averse to Thought
This Book is Dedicated
With Unfeigned Respect*

I am far from holding the opinion that a single life is
necessarily an unhappy life: there is too much reason to think
otherwise; but I am very desirous that its peculiar
disadvantages should be better understood, and rescued from
the exclusive service of would-be wit; and I believe that those
who feel them most bitterly will forgive a recognition of these
disadvantages, if they agree with me in thinking that an evil,

clearly defined, is, far less formidable than that which has the painful honour of being indescribable. . . .

There are many who have chosen single life with deliberate preference, and who wonder at the vulgar error of supposing that *every* woman would be happier married, and that every woman has wished to be so.

*   *   *

MARJORIE S. BROUGHALL

Pastel for Eliza, 1961

"The young lady of the 1850's"

The young lady of the 1850's, once released from the schoolroom, seems to have had a good deal of time at her own disposal. She might be trained by her mother in the sensible and profitable use of it, "improving it" as the phrase was; but with that mother ruling the house and servants doing the work, and with no profession of her own to claim the most vigorous hours of every day, she had no satisfaction of powers at stretch, and only too much leisure. In a small family she could often "retire" to her own room, a privacy denied to larger families, to read, to meditate, to day-dream. Eliza did all three.

"I have many opportunities now for retirement," she recorded in her diary at eighteen, and added "I feel that my great temptation is in giving way to vain and trifling thoughts. I am surprised on looking back at the close of the day to find how much of my time has been spent in this way."

There were so few openings for women at that time that even the scope of day-dreams was limited. Eliza seems to have fashioned for herself two roles, that of the happy wife and mother, held out as goal to all Victorian misses, and that of the successful writer. The former, though blessed by society, had its dangers, especially if the dream began to twine itself prematurely round some particular gentleman. So indulged it might bring disillusion and shame and self-reproach. But was not the other dream mere vanity? Day-dreams in fact were sinful, at any rate for her, Eliza decided. Yet how could anyone with no responsibilities, with few duties and those largely self-imposed, fill the mind's vacuum except with sinful dreams? Eliza faced the question and found a practical answer. Instead of sitting idly she would choose 'some useful subject' and write down her thoughts about it. While she sewed - much mechanical needlework was included in a girl's lot - she could develop her ideas. She tried the plan: she wrote down reflections on the way in which a girl who has emerged from the schoolroom should persevere with her own education, a relevant topic. Her thoughts came readily; her pen coursed over the paper. The result pleased her. She copied it out and sent it to the *British Mothers' Magazine.* To her delight, first effort though it was, it was accepted. Eliza at nineteen had founded one of her castles on the ground. She was a writer.

*   *   *

CHARLES DICKENS, 1812 - 1870

Great Expectations, 1861

"Papa wants me, darling!"
Herbert had told me on former occasions, and now reminded me, that he first knew Miss Clara Barley when she was completing her education at an establishment at Hammersmith, and that on her being recalled home to nurse her father, he and she had confided their affection to the motherly Mrs. Whimple, by whom it had been fostered and regulated with equal kindness and discretion, ever since. It was understood that nothing of a tender nature could possibly be confided to Old Barley, by reason of his being totally unequal to the consideration of any subject more psychological than Gout, Rum, and Purser's stores.
As we were thus conversing in a low tone while Old Barley's sustained growl vibrated in the beam that crossed the ceiling, the room door opened, and a very pretty, slight, dark-eyed girl of twenty or so, came in with a basket in her hand: whom

Herbert tenderly relieved of the basket, and presented blushing, as "Clara." She really was a most charming girl, and might have passed for a captive fairy, whom that truculent Ogre, Old Barley, had pressed into his service.

"Look here," said Herbert, showing me that basket, with a compassionate and tender smile after we had talked a little; "here's poor Clara's supper, served out every night. Here's her allowance of bread, and here's her slice of cheese, and here's her rum - which I drink. This is Mr. Barley's breakfast for to-morrow, served out to be cooked. Two mutton chops, three potatoes, some split peas, a little flour, two ounces of butter, a pinch of salt, and all this black pepper. It's stewed up together, and taken hot, and its a nice thing for the gout, I should think!"

There was something so natural and winning in Clara's resigned way of looking at these stores in detail, as Herbert pointed them out - and something so confiding, loving, and innocent, in her modest manner of yielding herself to Herbert's embracing arm - and something so gentle in her, so much needing protection on Mill Pond Bank, by Chinks's Basin, and the Old Green Copper Rope-Walk, with Old Barley growling in the beam - that I would not have undone the engagement between her and Herbert, for all the money in the pocket-book I had never opened.

I was looking at her with pleasure and admiration, when suddenly the growl swelled into a roar again, and a frightful bumping noise was heard above, as if a giant with a wooden leg were trying to bore it through the ceiling to come at us. Upon this Clara said to Herbert, "Papa wants me, darling!" and ran away.

"There is an unconscionable old shark for you!" said Herbert. "What do you suppose he wants now, Handel?" "I don't know," said I. "Something to drink?"

"That's it!" cried Herbert, as if I had made a guess of extraordinary merit. "He keeps his grog ready-mixed in a little tub on the table. Wait a moment, and you'll hear Clara lift him up to take some. - There he goes!" Another roar, with a prolonged shake at the end. "Now," said Herbert, as it was succeeded by silence, "he's drinking. Now," said Herbert, as the growl resounded in the beam once more, "he's down again on his back!"

JOSEPHINE KAMM

How Different from Us, 1958

Schoolgirl Fashions in the 1870's
She did not envy the "Myra" girls for the loose, warm
clothing they had to wear or for the ban which Miss Buss had
placed on tight lacing and stiff stays. As a growing girl in the
1870s she wore three petticoats - flannel, quilted eiderdown
and *moire;* and in order to acquire the fashionable tiny waist
her stays and skirt-bands were as tight as she dared to make
them without incurring Miss Buss's active displeasure. The
model of an "'ideal" maiden with an ample waist' which Miss
Buss had had made as an example and displayed in the school
had small appeal, although in winter the girls were often
miserably uncomfortable. "All our dresses had short sleeves,
and we were wretchedly cold and had chilblained fingers. We
had muslin sleeves that we put on when we went out: elastic at
the tops, generally much too tight - no sort of warm knickers,
only linen drawers, and later on, promotion to 'open drawers'
made like combinations."
Frances Mary - and Dorothea also -waged continuous warfare
against unsuitable clothing, rich food and unhygienic
conditions. "I hope your daughter wears woollen combinations in winter", Miss Buss told a mother who had come to
discuss her daughter's examination prospects (as the daughter
recalled in 1950). "That is of more importance to her than
passing Matriculation." And she asked parents to provide
their daughters with thick-soled warm house-boots to wear in
the uncarpeted school passages. In 1874 she was complaining
to Miss Davies of the prejudice they still had to endure on the
score of health. "Girton suffers largely, I believe, from the
determined opposition of medical men, and as for me, I
scarcely expect anything else if a medical opinion be asked, in
the case of any girl. The smallest ailment always proceeds
from over-brainwork!!! Never from neglected conditions of
health, from too many parties, etc. etc."
At Cheltenham Dorothea was extremely vexed when she found
that the parents of any of the day-girls were disregarding the
obvious laws of health. "Some of the things we should insist on
most strongly", she said in an address to parents, "would be a

ban on late evening work, an insistence on eight hours' sleep and no work or exercise directly after a meal. . . ."

Cotton dresses should not be worn in the spring or autumn; and every girl should be inspected before she left home to make sure that she was suitably dressed and, if necessary, carried a waterproof and umbrella. Girls were apt to be careless about putting on a wrap when coming out of church or a concert room; "and if I may express an opinion, it will be very unfavourable to the fashionable boa, which tends to produce sore throat by unduly heating it". She would, she added, be very glad to arrange a course of lectures on hygiene with special reference to the health of girls.

*   *   *

ELIZABETH S. HALDANE, 1862 - 1937

From One Century to Another, 1937

Election of the first Edinburgh school board, c. 1872
The four sturdy brothers and above all the medical tutor were violently against women coming into universities. I do not remember what they thought of "public life" in so far as serving on public boards was concerned, probably they did not think at all. Our parents were so engrossed in religious matters that such things did not seem to concern them. One of the lady candidates (the word "woman" was never, of course, used) was a Miss Flora Stevenson much respected by all Edinburgh society despite her being considered somewhat "advanced" in her views. Now it struck me, could I help this lady's candidature? It seemed difficult, but I had an idea, for I knew that each householder had as many votes as there were candidates and even if I could secure one it would be a brave deed. At that time my father was suffering from headache and he liked me to sit by him and stroke his hair to set him to sleep. I waited till he was not quite asleep but, as I thought, in a peaceful state of mind, and then I screwed up my courage and said, "Papa, do you think you would mind giving *one* of your votes to Miss Stevenson?" I can still remember the start

of the peaceful papa, right out of his chair. "What is the child speaking of?" he exclaimed in amazement. The world to him was evidently turning upside down, and so in fact it was. . . .

The Misses Stevenson
Later on I came to know the Misses Stevenson who worked so valiantly for the cause. They were four attractive and wealthy ladies who, still young, managed to elude all suitors; and as they occupied a large house near ours, we knew them by sight: later on they became real and valued friends with whom I often stayed. Miss Flora, the ablest and essentially a woman of the world, never failed to be elected for the school board and for long was its distingished chairman. Her name is perpetuated in an Edinburgh school. Louisa, also a clever woman, worked for women's education and arranged for classes for women of University standing, before women were admitted within the University portals, as well as helping to set on foot a school for domestic science. Another sister was artistic and did much for the Kyrle Society, like Miranda Hill, Octavia's sister, while the last was housekeeper and kept all the domestic wheels running smoothly.

*　　*　　*

VICTORIA   GLENDINNING

A Suppressed Cry, 1969
Life and Death of a Quaker Daughter

Winnie Seebohm of Hitchin, 1863 - 1885

Visit   away from home, 1880
In 1880, when she was seventeen, life began to open out a bit for Winnie. Being a Quaker, there was no question of "coming out", but she began to go away on visits, see new places, and meet people unconnected with the little Hitchin world. The Seebohm girls' growing-up process was accelerated by their mother's delicate health. The necessity for her to lead what was commonly called a "sofa life" meant that the daughters took over some of her duties. Juliet from about 1879

142

frequently acted as substitute hostess, and was in charge of the Dinner Book, an exercise book in which she recorded who came to dinner and what they ate. (A typical dinner, given for Professor Vinogradoff in 1883, consisted of clear soup, cod, oyster patties, chicken quenelles, roast beef, partridges, corbeilles de creme, Victoria custard and cheese ramakins). It also meant that one or other of the daughters very often took the place of their mother at Papa's side on his many visits to places and people of interest.

The first time Winnie went on a visit quite alone was to her aunt and uncle Barclay at their house in Brighton - one of their daughters, May, was about her age. On the first night away from home she sat up in bed and wrote Hugh (her brother) an ecstatic account of the delights provided in the guest bedroom:

Four boxes jujubes;
One plate grapes;
Two bone spoons;
One tin biscuits;
One glass coffee;
One glass barley-water;
Four blankets;
One quilt;
Two shawls;
One fire;
One hot-water bottle;
Two maids to wait upon a poor creature who got rid of them as soon as possible!

The first denial: to marriage
There is one letter which, though mutilated, escaped destruction . . . written on February 5th 1886, about six weeks after Winnie's death. It provides the only clue to what happened in 1882. . .

"She certainly would not have been strong enough to have met the strain of all that - neither the pains nor the joys of married life . . . Papa was right."

Newnham - to go up or not to go up?

"It was in January 1885" wrote Esther the recording angel, "that Winnie first made known her wish to go to Newnham. An alteration then made in family plans led her for the first time to feel she could be spared from home. It is evident that her object in wishing to go was not mere enjoyment, but the desire to fit herself for possible usefulness in after life. As Hugh was going to Cambridge in October this seemed the natural time for her to begin too".

Winnie was tired of waiting for life to begin. She decided to take matters into her own hands, and she wanted Meta to do likewise and come with her. Mr. Tuke was away from home at the time, so Meta took the decision to begin studying for the Cambridge Higher Local Examination (the entrance qualification for Newnham) on her own and in secret. When Mr. Tuke came home and was tentatively informed of his daughter's plans, he was not at all pleased. There were special reasons for this. Business relations between Mr. Tuke and Winnie's Papa were rather strained, owing to Frederic's political aspirations and subsequent frustration. And Newnham, because it was undenominational, had a name for being the cradle for free-thinkers. There were quarrels and reproaches. . . .

Newnham achieved - though not for long

Winnie heard that she had got a distinction in both Literature papers, and second-class Honours in German and French. A note came from Miss Clough offering her a place at Newnham. Winnie had done it - and for her there was no question of turning the offer down. She wrote to her cousin in Australia:

Unless I go now I certainly shall *never* go to Newnham, and I have never in my life had any first-rate teaching. I shall, I hope, be more fit for teaching (or any other work) after a year or two of study there. And in my next I shall be able to give you a description of College life and the effects of "Higher Education" upon the women of this generation!!. . .

And she wrote to Miss Clough to accept the place for the

coming October, and to Miss Helen Gladstone the Vice-Principal (daughter of the Prime Minister) to confirm that she would like to be in residence in the North Hall. . . .
But Winnie was not long enough at Newnham to make many very close relationships. She went up on October 10th 1885 and left again on November 12th.

The second denial: to independence

Winnie's letter-writing was interrupted at this point by a visit from Hugh who had just been home for the weekend. He told her that the family thought she was too ill to go on at Newnham, and that she must come home almost at once. Papa was coming over with Esther on Monday, the following day, to arrange about her departure. They had already written to Miss Clough.

What happened in fact was that Papa came up alone on the Monday and talked Winnie into agreement. She actually left Newnham on Wednesday.

After Hugh had left her, Winnie finished her letter to Juliet.

Hugh has just been up and I don't know what to think. . . .Dr. Paget *said* I was better, and I'm not working the least bit hard - and now I've got rid of asthma I shall get on. I *wish* you had written to me first before writing to Miss Clough and all - I can't bear to see her until we have talked and fixed, and it will just make her anxious - she will send for me to go down and I shan't know what to say. . . .

This is written in a great hurry before post goes. My spirits had risen after Friday's report - tho' they weren't low before by any means.

Winnie's memo book, late that same night

In case I should ever be tempted to regret my desire to come to Newnham and doubt my motives, I want to write them down as I honestly conceive them.

My first object was to learn history well and thoroughly, that I might be able (should I prove capable later) to write it for the working classes.

Secondly, I thought after a year or two here I should be better able to judge whether I was likely to be capable of any work of this sort.

Thirdly, I hoped to learn here self-reliance, judgement and self-confidence.

I am quite sure that I never cared a bit about the examinations, and I do not think I ever counted much upon the enjoyments here - certainly not when I actually came. I looked upon the life here as the best preparation within my reach for the work which I hoped someday to spend my life over. And I thought it was perhaps as well that the enjoyment should be put out of my reach, for fear I might forget the definite purposes for which I came.

The victim of a system - and it is still happening

Nobody could have been more loved in life than Winnie. But it is a sad fact that the love of parents, brothers and sisters, is not enough to give life a shape for most adults. Winnie was the victim of a system: there were hundreds in the same predicament before her, and it is still happening all the time. Mostly the victims smoulder on, but Winnie's bonfire was completely doused. Winnie died.

Why did she have to die? Her asthma killed her. Why did she have such asthma?

*   *   *

OSCAR WILDE, 1854 - 1900

The Importance of Being Earnest, 1895

Gwendolen. I adore you. But you haven't proposed to me yet. Nothing has been said at all about marriage. The subject has not even been touched on.

Jack. Well . . . may I propose to you now?

Gwendolen. I think it would be an admirable opportunity. And to spare you any possible disappointment, Mr. Worthing, I think it is only fair to tell you quite frankly beforehand that I am determined to accept you.

Jack. Gwendolen!

146

Gwendolen. Yes, Mr. Worthing, what have you got to say to me?

Jack. You know what I have got to say to you.

Gwendolen. Yes, but you don't say it.

Jack. Gwendolen, will you marry me?

(Goes on his knees.)

Gwendolen. Of course I will, darling. How long you have been about it! I am afraid you have had very little experience in how to propose.

Jack. My own one, I have never loved any one in the world but you.

Gwendolen. Yes, but men often propose for practice. I know my brother Gerald does. All my girl-friends tell me so. What wonderfully blue eyes you have, Ernest! They are quite, quite blue. I hope you will always look at me just like that, especially when there are other people present.

(Enter Lady Bracknell.)

Lady Bracknell. Mr. Worthing! Rise, sir, from this semi-recumbent posture. It is most indecorous.

Gwendolen. Mamma! *(He tries to rise; she restrains him.)* I must beg you to retire. This is no place for you. Besides, Mr. Worthing has not quite finished yet.

Lady Bracknell. Finished what, may I ask?

Gwendolen. I am engaged to Mr. Worthing, mamma.

(They rise together.)

Lady Bracknell. Pardon me, you are not engaged to any one. When you do become engaged to some one, I, or your father, should his health permit him, will inform you of the fact. An engagement should come on a young girl as a surprise, pleasant or unpleasant, as the case may be. It is hardly a matter that she could be allowed to arrange for herself. . . . And now I have a few questions to put to you, Mr. Worthing. While I am making these inquiries, you, Gwendolen, will wait for me below in the carriage.

Gwendolen (reproachfully). Mamma!

Lady Bracknell. In the carriage, Gwendolen!

(Gwendolen goes to the door. She and Jack blow kisses to each other behind Lady Bracknell's back. Lady Bracknell looks vaguely about as if she could not understand what the noise was. Finally turns round.)

Gwendolen, the carriage!

Gwendolen. Yes, mamma.

(Goes out, looking back at Jack.)

Lady Bracknell (sitting down). You can take a seat, Mr. Worthing.

(Looks in her pocket for notebook and pencil.)

Jack. Thank you, Lady Bracknell, I prefer standing.

Lady Bracknell (pencil and notebook in hand). I feel bound to tell you that you are not down on my list of eligible young men, although I have the same list as the dear Duchess of Bolton has. We work together, in fact. However, I am quite ready to enter your name, should your answers be what a really affectionate mother requires. Do you smoke?

Jack. Well, yes, I must admit I smoke.

Lady Bracknell. I am glad to hear it. A man should always have an occupation of some kind. There are far too many idle men in London as it is. How old are you?

Jack. Twenty-nine.

Lady Bracknell. A very good age to be married at. I have always been of opinion that a man who desires to get married should know either everything or nothing. Which do you know?

Jack (after some hesitation). I know nothing, Lady Bracknell.

Lady Bracknell. I am pleased to hear it. I do not approve of anything that tampers with natural ignorance. Ignorance is like a delicate exotic fruit; touch it and the bloom is gone. The whole theory of modern education is radically unsound. Fortunately in England, at any rate, education produces no effect whatsoever. If it did, it would prove a serious danger to the upper classes, and probably lead to acts of violence in Grosvenor Square. What is your income?

Jack. Between seven and eight thousand a year.

Lady Bracknell (makes a note in her book). In land, or in investments?

Jack. In investments, chiefly.

Lady Bracknell. That is satisfactory. What between the duties expected of one during one's lifetime, and the duties exacted from one after one's death, land has ceased to be either a profit or a pleasure. It gives one position, and prevents one from keeping it up. That's all that can be said about land.

Jack. I have a country house with some land, of course,

attached to it - about fifteen hundred acres, I believe; but I don't depend on that for my real income. In fact, as far as I can make out, the poachers are the only people who make anything out of it.

Lady Bracknell. A country house! How many bedrooms? Well that point can be cleared up afterwards. You have a town house, I hope? A girl with a simple, unspoiled nature, like Gwendolen, could hardly be expected to reside in the country.

Jack. Well, I own a house in Belgrave Square, but it is let by the year to Lady Bloxham. Of course, I can get it back whenever I like, at six months' notice.

Lady Bracknell. Lady Bloxham? I don't know her.

Jack. Oh, she goes about very little. She is a lady considerably advanced in years.

Lady Bracknell. Ah, nowadays that is no guarantee of respectability of character. What number in Belgrave Square?

Jack. 149.

Lady Bracknell (shaking her head). The unfashionable side. I thought there was something. However, that could easily be altered.

Jack. Do you mean the fashion, or the side?

Lady Bracknell (sternly). Both, if necessary, I presume. What are your politics?

Jack. Well, I am afraid I really have none. I am a Liberal Unionist.

Lady Bracknell. Oh, they count as Tories. They dine with us. Or come in the evening, at any rate. Now to minor matters. Are your parents living?

Jack. I have lost both my parents.

Lady Bracknell. Both? . . . That seems like carelessness. Who was your father? He was evidently a man of some wealth. Was he born in what the Radical papers call the purple of commerce, or did he rise from the ranks of the aristocracy?

*Jack.*I am afraid I really don't know. The fact is, Lady Bracknell, I said I had lost my parents. It would be nearer the truth to say that my parents seem to have lost me. . . . I don't actually know who I am by birth. I was . . . well, I was found.

Lady Bracknell. Found!

Jack. The late Mr. Thomas Cardew, an old gentleman of a very charitable and kindly disposition, found me, and gave me the name of Worthing, because he happened to have a first-class ticket for Worthing in his pocket at the time. Worthing is a place in Sussex. It is a seaside resort.

Lady Bracknell. Where did the charitable gentleman who had a first-class ticket for this seaside resort find you?

Jack (gravely). In a hand-bag.

Lady Bracknell. A hand-bag?

Jack (very seriously). Yes, Lady Bracknell. I was in a hand-bag - a somewhat large, black leather hand-bag, with handles to it - an ordinary hand-bag in fact.

Lady Bracknell. In what locality did this Mr. James, or Thomas Cardew come across this ordinary hand-bag?

Jack. In the cloakroom at Victoria Station. It was given to him in mistake for his own.

Lady Bracknell. The cloakroom at Victoria Station?

Jack. Yes. The Brighton line.

Lady Bracknell. The line is immaterial. Mr. Worthing, I confess I feel somewhat bewildered by what you have just told me. To be born, or at any rate bred, in a hand-bag, whether it had handles or not, seems to me to display a contempt for the ordinary decencies of family life that reminds one of the worst excesses of the French Revolution. And I presume you know what that unfortunate movement led to? As for the particular locality in which the hand-bag was found, a cloakroom at a railway station might serve to conceal a social indiscretion - has probably, indeed, been used for that purpose before now - but it could hardly be regarded as an assured basis for a recognized position in good society.

Jack. May I ask you then what you would advise me to do? I need hardly say I would do anything in the world to ensure Gwendolen's happiness.

Lady Bracknell. I would strongly advise you, Mr. Worthing, to try and acquire some relations as soon as possible, and to make a definite effort to produce at any rate one parent, of either sex, before the season is quite over.

Jack. Well, I don't see how I could possibly manage to do that. I can produce the hand-bag at any moment. It is in my dressing-room at home. I really think that should satisfy you, Lady Bracknell.

Lady Bracknell. Me, sir! What has it to do with me? You can hardly imagine that I and Lord Bracknell would dream of allowing our only daughter - a girl brought up with the utmost care - to marry into a cloakroom, and form an alliance with a

parcel. Good morning Mr. Worthing!
(Lady Bracknell sweeps out in majestic indignation).

*   *   *

HARRY GRAHAM, 1874 - 1936

The Bath

> Broad is the Gate and wide the Path
> That leads man to his daily bath;
> But ere you spend the shining hour
> With plunge and spray, with sluice and show'r -
> With all that teaches you to dread
> The bath as little as your bed -
> Remember, whereso'er you be,
> To shut the door and turn the key.
>
> I had a friend - my friend no more -
> Who failed to bolt the bath-room door;
>
> A maiden aunt of his, one day,
> Walked in, as half-submerged he lay.
>
> She did not notice nephew John,
> And turned the boiling water on.
>
> He had no time, nor even scope,
> To camouflage himself with soap,
> But gave a yell and flung aside
> The sponge 'neath which he sought to hide.
>
> It fell to earth I know not where.
> He beat his breast in his despair,
>
> And then, like Venus from the foam,
> Sprang into view, and made for home.

151

His aunt fell fainting to the ground.
Alas! they never brought her round.

She died, intestate, in her prime,
The victim of another's crime;

And John can never quite forget
How, by a breach of etiquette,
He lost, at one fell swoop (or plunge),
His aunt, his honour, and his sponge.

13

TWENTIETH CENTURY

ELLEN DOROTHY ABB

If she still feels a bit sore about missing marriage, she can always console herself, if she looks round at some of the women who marry and some of the men they marry, that after all it can't be so hard to find a husband; must just be that she hadn't the knack. Like not having a light hand with pastry.

*   *   *

CICELY HAMILTON, 1872 - 1952

Marriage as a Trade, 1909

I do not advocate celibacy except for persons whom it suits; but I do not see why persons whom it does suit should be ashamed of acknowledging the fact. I am inclined to think that they are more numerous than is commonly supposed, and I will admit frankly that I am exceedingly glad that it seems, in these latter days, to suit so many women. I am glad, not because the single life appears to me essentially better than the married, but because I believe that the conditions of marriage, as they affect women, can only be improved by the women who do without marriage - and do without it gladly.

*   *   *

WALTER DE LA MARE, 1873-1956

The Listeners and Other Poems, 1912

Miss Loo

When thin-strewn memory I look through,
I see most clearly poor Miss Loo;
Her tabby cat, her cage of birds,
Her nose, her hair, her muffled words,
And how she'd open her green eyes,
As if in some immense surprise,
Whenever as we sat at tea
She made some small remark to me.
It's always drowsy summer when
From out the past she comes again;
The westering sunshine in a pool
Floats in her parlour still and cool;
While the slim bird its lean wires shakes,
As into piercing song it breaks;

Till Peter's pale-green eyes ajar
Dream, wake; wake, dream, in one brief bar.
And I am sitting, dull and shy,
And she with gaze of vacancy,
And large hands folded on the tray,
Musing the afternoon away;
Her satin bosom heaving slow
With sighs that softly ebb and flow,
And her plain face in such dismay,
It seems unkind to look her way:
Until all cheerful back will come
Her gentle gleaming spirit home:
And one would think that poor Miss Loo
Asked nothing else, if she had you.

*   *   *

THE TIMES, 19th APRIL 1914

The Vampire On The Hearth
A Plea For The Victims

(From a Correspondent)
Every day a host of human vampires drain the life-blood of
those who are their nearest and should be their dearest. They
have no seductive graces. Their limbs are not sinuous, nor
their lips scarlet. Sometimes, like the monsters of the legends,
they are men, sometimes, though not often, they are young.
But as a rule the most noxious specimens of the common
house-vampire are old ladies, apparently, you would say, quite
nice old ladies, incapable of hurting a fly. But the poison of
asps is under their lips, and they are all true to type in being
the ghosts of their former selves.
The most usual species is the widowed mother with a daughter
of any age from 20 to 50. The other children have gone out
into the world to marry and to work, and incidentally to live
their own lives in homes of their own. Clearly it is the duty of
the one who is left to look after the little mother. That is the
universal verdict of the world and the family. If she submits, if
she sacrifices her youth and her individuality on the altar of
the Fifth Commandment, her doom is sealed. The longer she
stays on with her mother the more impossible it is for her to
break away. Day and night she is at her beck and call. Her
opinions, her gifts, her ambitions she must keep in the
background till they atrophy from want of use. She must come
when she is called, go where she is sent, walk or drive cheek by
jowl with the vampire who saps her vitality, write her letters,
pay calls, "do" the flowers, exercise the dog, order the dinner,
pay the wages, engage and dismiss her servants, count the
linen, keep the books, and, to speak generally, run the house
for the vampire's convenience from the vampire's point of
view, without any regard to her own inclinations, and, as often
as not, on lines of which she does not approve. In everything
she is treated as a child who has never grown up.

Spoilt And Wasted Lives
The whole of such a life is the perfect realisation (and the
practical negation) of the theory that the proper sphere of
woman is the home. If it were her own home - but then it is

not, and that makes all the difference. Year after year, from January to December, she plays the part of daughter, companion, hospital nurse, housekeeper, accountant, amanuensis, and general factotum and slave, with no thanks, no wages, no holidays, and nothing to look forward to but a release for which she cannot pray. In course of time it may come, but too late probably to be of any use, when her life is sucked dry, and body, soul, and spirit, she is broken and withered.

This is not an exaggerated picture. Most of us can match it from our own experience. London is full of girls and women of gentle birth, living very often on the merest pittance, who have deliberately cut themselves adrift from such an existence as this and asserted their right to be themselves, no matter at what cost. But their unhappy stay-at-home sisters are Andromedas who grow old before their time, wearily waiting for the Perseus who never comes. For them there is no escape. The vampire ("Such a devoted mother, my dear!") has them by the throat, and slowly but surely squeezes the life out of them and drains them of youth and joy and hope. In all the long catalogue of woman's real and fancied woes there is hardly one more infuriating and none more depressing to contemplate than the commonplace tragedies of these spoilt and wasted lives.

*　　*　　*

THE TIMES, APRIL 15 1971

A Remarkable View Of Front-Line Service In Imperial Russia First exhibition of souvenirs and photographs collected by nurse

From Christopher Walker, Heswall, Cheshire, April 14
Perhaps the most remarkable and original exhibition of imperial Russian souvenirs and photographs to be held in Britain will be opened officially here tomorrow night. All exhibits are the property of Miss Florence Farnborough, who will be celebrating her eighty-fifth birthday.

In an almost unbelievable life-time of adventure, Miss Farnborough was the only English nurse to serve with the Russian Red Cross through the First World War. She was also one of the early woman foreign correspondents of *The Times*, and the chief English language broadcaster on Franco's radio station during the Spanish Civil War.

One of a family of six, Miss Farnborough was named after Florence Nightingale. One of her earliest memories is of waving to that formidable woman through the window of a small cottage in Buckinghamshire.

She first went to live in Russia in 1908, when she was 21.

The centrepiece of the exhibition is a collection of nearly 700 photographs which she took during her time as one of four nurses in the first flying column of the 10th Field (Surgical) Unit of the Russian Red Cross. Most of them have never been shown in public and would do credit to any contemporary war photographer.

"At the time, I didn't realize their historical significance", she said today. "I just felt that the world around me was so interesting that I must snap it while I could."

The photographs show many sides of the war, and of the first months of the Russian revolution. "No one seemed to mind me being there photographing what they were doing," said Miss Farnborough, who remains modest about her achievements. Many publishers have tried to persuade her to write a book, but she has always refused.

Fluent in six languages, she moved to Moscow in 1910 to live in the house of a heart surgeon, Dr. P. Ousoff. At the outbreak of war, she received a cable from her parents saying: "Do not dream of coming home. The war will never last more than four months." Instead, she joined the Russian Red Cross and, after six months training, was sent to the Galician Front. Throughout the war she was never more than a few miles from the front line, always with camera in hand.

She is unwilling to talk much of her personal relationships, or of her reasons for not marrying. "I almost did marry a Russian once, but perhaps it was for the best that I never did," she said.

The exhibition includes a large number of colourful letters from Russian soldiers thanking her for her work during the war.

For her services she received, among other honours, two

medals from the Tsar. Nostalgically, she likes to remember that these still entitle her to a small annual pension from the old imperialist government.

Miss Farnborough's photographs more than illustrate the dangers in which she lived during the three and a half years as the only English woman on the Russian front. Among other unique documents, she also has an original of a little-known manifesto issued by Tsar Nicholas II, handing over the throne to his brother, the Grand Duke Michael. Dated March 2, 1917, the manifesto was circulated to a select few.

Her own unit, known as Letouchka - the flying ambulance - was disbanded in January, 1918. At the beginning of March she left Moscow with a party of British refugees and spent 27 days in a cattle truck travelling through Siberia to Vladivostok. She then lived in the truck on a siding for three more weeks, before being rescued.

When she eventually returned to England, Miss Farnborough contributed a number of articles to *The Times.* The first, which appeared on July 13, 1918, went under the heading: "Moscow as it is, picture of Soviet misrule."

Eight years ago, as a tourist, she paid her first and only return visit to the U.S.S.R. "I admit I was biased, but I was also amazed", she reflects. "I could never have believed that so much good could have come out of so much evil. The idea of the brotherhood of man was a great thing, but I would never have thought it could have been brought about by violence and bloodshed."

*   *   *

VOTES FOR WOMEN, MAY 17, 1912

Miss Horniman, pioneer of the Repertory Theatre
The theatre I took at Manchester lost its license in the days of its unfortunate "past", but I ran it so respectably I proved that a middle-aged suburban spinster can run a theatre in a decent manner, so I got the excise license.

*   *   *

T. S. ELIOT, 1888 - 1965

Prufrock, 1917

Aunt Helen

Miss Helen Slingsby was my maiden aunt,
And lived in a small house near a fashionable square
Cared for by servants to the number of four.
Now when she died there was silence in heaven
And silence at her end of the street.
The shutters were drawn and the undertaker wiped his feet -
He was aware that this sort of thing had occurred before.
The dogs were handsomely provided for,
But shortly afterwards the parrot died too.
The Dresden clock continued ticking on the mantelpiece,
And the footman sat upon the dining-table
Holding the second housemaid on his knees -
Who had always been so careful while her mistress lived.

Cousin Nancy

Miss Nancy Ellicott
Strode across the hills and broke them,
Rode across the hills and broke them -
The barren New England hills -
Riding to hounds
Over the cow-pasture.

Miss Nancy Ellicott smoked
And danced all the modern dances;
And her aunts were not quite sure how they felt about it,
But they knew that it was modern.

Upon the glazen shelves kept watch
Matthew and Waldo, guardians of the faith,
The army of unalterable law.

CLEMENCE DANE, 1891 - 1965

The Woman's Side, 1926

"The law of numbers is against her"

Very different is the sex problem for the unmarried business woman, the woman so often and so insultingly called "superfluous". Here you have the problem, inevitable in a country where monogamy is the custom and where women greatly outnumber men, of sex in the unmarried girl. The girl who doesn't marry (except in rare cases usually balanced by equivalent rare cases among men) is in no way different, physically, mentally, emotionally, from the girl who does marry. The law of numbers is against her, nothing else.

*　　*　　*

A. P. HERBERT, 1890 - 1973

She Shanties, 1926

I Wouldn't Be Too Lady-like

I wouldn't be too lady-like in love if I were you.
I used to sit in this here park with somebody I knew;
And he was very fond of me, and I was fond of Joe,
And yet we got no forrarder in seven years or so.

> Well, he'd sit thinking, "Do I dare?"
> And I'd sit thinking, "Lord, he's slow!"
> And so we both sat thinking there,
> And then it would be time to go.
> I only had to say, "Oh, Joe . . .!"
> And he'd have kissed me, that I know;
> But could I do it? I could not.
> And so he married Mabel Bott -
> And all because I acted like a lady.

Some days we used to sit at home and talk about the rain;
I've always heard that perfect love made everything so plain;
They may be right - all I can say, I never found it so,
For Love is just about the biggest muddle that I know.

> Well, dear, he loved me in his way,
> And I was very fond of Joe,
> But he was too afraid to say,
> And I was too refined to show.
> And just when things were shaping well
> Mamma came in and broke the spell;
> It broke his spirit in the end,
> He went and found another friend -
> And all because I acted like a lady.

I blame it on my mother, dear, who brought me up too well.
And told me when a girl was kissed a girl should ring the bell.
We women mustn't take the lead, but now and then you'll find
It's just as well to give a man a little push behind.

> Well, he'd sit thinking, "Do I dare?"
> And I'd sit thinking, "Go it, Joe!"
> And so we just sat thinking there,
> And then, it seemed, he had to go.
> I only had to catch his eye,
> And sigh a sort of sickly sigh;
> But could I do it? I could not.
> And so he married Mabel Bott -
> And all because I acted like a lady.

Ballads for Broadbrows, 1930

Other People's Babies
A Song Of Kensington Gardens

Babies? It's a gift, my dear; and I should say I know,
For I've been pushing prams about for forty years or so;
Thirty-seven babies - or is it thirty-nine?
No, I'm wrong; it's thirty-six - but none of them was mine.

161

Other people's babies -
That's my life!
Mother to dozens,
And nobody's wife.
But then it isn't everyone can say
They used to bath the Honourable Hay,
Lord James Montague, Sir Richard Twistle-Thynnes,
Captain Cartlet and the Ramrod twins.
Other people's babies,
Other people's prams,
Such little terrors,
Such little lambs!
Sixty-one today,
And ought to be a granny;
Sixty-one today,
And nothing but a Nanny!
There, ducky, there,
Did the lady stare?
Don't cry! Oh, my!
Other people's babies!

Everybody's told me, dear, since I was seventeen,
I ought to been a mother - what a mother I'd have been!
Mind you, minding babies isn't everybody's line,
But I wouldn't mind the minding, dear, if I was minding mine.

Other people's babies
All my life -
Three dozen mothers,
And not one wife.
Of course, it isn't everyone can say
They used to bath the Honourable Hay,
Lord Charles Cobley - had a present from the King -
And now, they tell me, he's a Bright Young Thing.
But forty years of bottles,
Forty years of fits,
Forty years of first teeth,
And here I sits,
Sixty-one today,
Might have been a granny,
Meant for a mother,
And nothing but a Nanny!

There, ducky, there,
Howl if you dare
Don't cry! Oh, my!
Other people's babies!

Isn't he a pet, my dear - the spit of Lady Stoop?
Looks a perfect picture, yes - I nursed him through the croup;
But I shall get my notice just as soon as he can crawl -
It's a funny thing to think he won't remember me at all.

Other people's babies,
Nothing to show -
Twelve months' trouble,
And out I go.
Of course, it isn't everyone can say
They used to bath the Honourable Hay,
Lady Susan Sparrow, what was dropped in the pond,
And now, Cook tells me, she's a well-known blonde.
But forty years of croup,
Forty years of frights,
Long, long days, dear,
And short, short nights -
Sixty-one today,
And ought to be a granny,
Pensions for the widows, eh?
But what about the Nanny?
There, ducky, there,
Nannies don't care!
Don't cry! Oh, my!
Other people's babies!

163

HILAIRE BELLOC, 1870 - 1953

New Cautionary Tales, 1930

Aunt Jane

"Mamma" said Amanda "I want to know what
Our relatives mean when they say
That Aunt Jane is a Gorgon who ought to be shot,
Or at any rate taken away.

"Pray what is a Gorgon and why do you shoot
It? Or are its advances refused?
Or is it perhaps a maleficent Brute?
I protest I am wholly bemused."

"The Term," said her Mother, "is certain to pain,
And is quite inexcusably rude.
Moreover Aunt Jane, though uncommonly plain,
Is also uncommonly good.

"She provides information without hesitation,
For people unwilling to learn;
And often bestows good advice upon those
Who give her no thanks in return.

"She is down before anyone's up in the place -
That is, up before anyone's down.
Her Domestics are awed by the shape of her face
And they tremble with fear at her frown.

"Her visiting list is of Clergymen who
Have reached a respectable age
And she pays her companion Miss Angela Drew
A sufficient and regular wage.

"Her fortune is large, though we often remark
On a modesty rare in the rich;
For her nearest and dearest are quite in the dark
As to what she will leave, or to which.

"Her conduct has ever been totally free
From censorious whispers of ill,
At any rate, since 1903 -
And probably earlier still.

"Your Father's dear sister presents in a word,
A model for all of her sex,
With a firmness of will that is never deterred,
And a confidence nothing can vex.

"I can only desire that you too should aspire
To such earthly reward as appears
In a high reputation, at present entire
After Heaven knows how many years.

"So in future remember to turn a deaf ear
To detraction - and now run away
To your brothers and sisters whose laughter I hear
In the garden below us at play."

"Oh, thank you, Mamma!" said Amanda at that,
And ran off to the innocent band
Who were merrily burying Thomas the Cat
Right up to his neck in the sand.

*   *   *

JOHN COWPER POWYS, 1872 - 1963

The Meaning of Culture, 1930

The importance of a room
Happy are those persons whose outward destiny leaves them at
least one solitary, independent room to retire to at night. It is a
pitiful and a wicked shame when young girls have to go on for
years and years living at home. It is easy for young men to
retain their individuality and live a life of culture in their
parents' dwellings: it is almost impossible for a girl to do so.

165

There is something about the parental aura - however kind and unselfish her parents may be - that is deadly to a girl's nature; and as cruel to her culture as the most insidious drops of poison. Her parents indeed may be fussing anxiously about her chastity while they themselves are all the while murdering her noblest culture more wickedly and effectively than could the most treacherous of lovers!

One learns indeed from the subtle stories of Dorothy Richardson what exactly it is that a mother's influence does to a daughter's life. Every woman is a creator, in the sense of creating a kind of spiritual *ménage* round her, wherever she is. She does this as instinctively as a silk-worm spins its cocoon. But by a terrible and cruel law of Nature there cannot be two *ménages* under one ceiling; so when a girl lives with her mother the deep creative instinct within her, that instinct which is her inward destiny, that instinct which is the very material of her culture, is teased, suppressed, tantalized, unsatisfied.

Even so - for "old maids" under certain conditions can be the most cultured persons of all - an unmarried woman living with her mother can, by sheer intellectual and imaginative power, liberate herself while she is still enslaved. But she must fight tooth and nail for a room entirely her own - never entered by her mother - and for the right to retire to this room as often as she pleases.

*   *   *

ROSAMUND LEHMANN

Invitation to the Waltz, 1932

The door was opened by old Mrs. Robinson: toothless, scored with wrinkles, exhaling the curious smell of an old woman. . . . I hate her, thought Olivia, left alone. It was the same catalogue of complaints every time. The Robinsons vied with each other in chronic suffering. The air in the house was heavy, lugubrious with their minor afflictions. But old Mrs. Robinson and the eldest daughter (the one whose weakness was in the head, who never appeared and never did anything) and the second daughter (the Post Office one) had a store of meek and voluptuous Christian patience on which to nourish disease; and the youngest, the dressmaking Miss Robinson, had none. She had only her imagination. . . .

The youngest Miss Robinson, gay-hearted, quivering, hysterical, started away now and then from the odour of complacent dejection and sanctified decay; but she could escape no further than to the front room and the twanging piano and the wild warbling of voluptuous ballads. This room, called now the fitting-room, she had won for herself: these four walls held the remnants of her freedom, her humour, her hope, like a wistful and dwindling presence within them. For she was sinking, fatally enmeshed, struggling feebly and more feebly as youth slipped from her year after year, and old Mrs. Robinson continued to be alive, and virginity, like a malignant growth, gnawed at her mind and body.

Why shouldn't Miss Robinson get married? Though plain, she was prettier than some, she loved a joke, could play the piano and sing, was domesticated, warm-hearted, good-tempered and generous, her nature craved affection. But she wouldn't get a husband: she hadn't a chance now. She was thirty. Letting I dare not wait upon I would, youth had gone by; and now the candour of her desires was muddied, her spark of spirit spent. Never would she do now what once she had almost done: walked out of the house and left them all whining and gone to London to earn her living. That was after the death of Mr. Robinson, an able cheerful man - manager of a department in the mills, churchwarden, clerk to the Parish Council. Though Connie said We must all look after Mother, now, and Gertie under emotional stress lost what head she had and needed special care, and Mother said I need all my dear daughters round me now, God willing we shall never part in this life, I feel it won't be long before I too Go Home - in spite of all this, she would - almost - have gone, and been the selfish one, the undutiful, the heartbreaker; and never come back to Little Compton again. But of course she hadn't done it. She didn't even know now that she disliked her mother. Enmeshed in those collapsible leather tentacles, she felt comfortable, developed poor health, had her nerves; went out only on Wednesday afternoons with Connie for a little shopping and perhaps the pictures in Tulverton: for they kept themselves to

167

themselves, finding, they said, all the society they wanted in their own home.

*   *   *

PADRAIC COLUM, 1881 - 1972

An Old Woman Of The Roads

O', to have a little house!
To own the hearth and stool and all!
The heaped-up sods upon the fire,
The pile of turf against the wall!

To have a clock with weights and chains
And pendulum swinging up and down!
A dresser filled with shining delph,
Speckled and white and blue and brown!

I could be busy all the day
Clearing and sweeping hearth and floor,
And fixing on their shelf again
My white and blue and speckled store!

I could be quiet there at night
Beside the fire and by myself,
Sure of a bed and loth to leave
The ticking clock and the shining delph!

Och! but I'm weary of mist and dark,
And roads where there's never a house nor bush
And tired I am of bog and road,
And the crying wind and the lonesome hush!

And I am praying to God on high,
And I am praying Him night and day,
For a little house - a house of my own -
Out of the wind's and the rain's way.

COLIN ELLIS, 1895 - 1969

Mournful Numbers, 1932

The Old Ladies

They walked in straitened ways,
They had not great possessions;
They lived before the days
When ladies learnt professions.

And one was rather mad
And äll were rather trying,
So little life they had,
So long they spent a-dying.

In spotless white lace caps,
Just sitting, sitting, sitting,
Their hands upon their laps
Or occupied with knitting.

And now they all are gone,
Miss Alice and Miss Ella,
Miss Jane (at ninety-one)
And poor Miss Arabella.

The house they loved so well
And always kept so nicely,
Some auctioneer will sell
"At six o'clock precisely".

It seemed as though their lives
Were wasted more than others',
They would have made good wives,
They might have made good mothers.

Yet this was their reward:
Through ninety years of leisure
Small precious things to guard,
None else had time to treasure.

Their crystal was their pride,
Their porcelain a token,
Kept safe until they died
And handed on unbroken.

*　　*　　*

GEORGE BERNARD SHAW, 1856 - 1950

The Adventures of the Black Girl in her Search for God, 1932

The missionary was a small white woman, not yet thirty: an odd little body who had found no satisfaction for her soul with her very respectable and fairly well-to-do family in her native England, and had settled down in the African forest to teach little African children to love Christ and adore the Cross. She was a born apostle of love. At school she had adored one or other of her teachers with an idolatry that was proof against all snubbing, but had never cared much for girls of her own age and standing. At eighteen she began falling in love with earnest clergymen, and actually became engaged to six of them in succession. But when it came to the point she always broke it off; for these love affairs, full at first of ecstatic happiness and hope, somehow became unreal and eluded her in the end. The clergymen thus suddenly and unaccountably disengaged did not always conceal their sense of relief and escape, as if they too had discovered that the dream was only a dream, or a sort of metaphor by which they had striven to express the real thing, but not itself the real thing.

One of the jilted, however, committed suicide; and this tragedy gave her an extraordinary joy. It seemed to take her from a fool's paradise of false happiness into a real region in which intense suffering became transcendent rapture.

But it put an end to her queer marriage engagements. Not that it was the last of them. But a worldly cousin, of whose wit she was a little afraid, and who roundly called her a coquette and a jilt, one day accused her of playing in her later engagements for another suicide, and told her that many a woman had been hanged for less. And though she knew in a way that this was

170

not true, and that the cousin, being a woman of this world, did not understand; yet she knew also that in the worldly way it was true enough, and that she must give up this strange game of seducing men into engagements which she now knew she would never keep. So she jilted the sixth clergyman and went to plant the cross in darkest Africa; and the last stirring in her of what she repudiated as sin was a flash of rage when he married the cousin, through whose wit and worldly wisdom he at last became a bishop in spite of himself.

*   *   *

ELLEN DOROTHY ABB

What Fools We Women Be, 1937

When we look back and see the achievements of the spinsters, it would be just as well if we belatedly gave them the thanks they rarely received at the time. We might also give an occasional appreciative thought to the unspectacular work of to-day's spinsters. Spinsters have eaten humble pie far too long. It may be love that makes the world go round, but it's spinsters who oil the wheels.
Where should we all be to-day without the teachers and nurses, those two classes of almost invariably celibate women?

All that these single women ask of life - by middle age at any rate - is liberty to go on working for long enough to give them food and shelter, warmth and clothes. A few odd shillings will cover their other requirements; they have long ago ceased to be exacting.
One wonders how many of them look back to the war with the same feelings as the ex-service men: "Well, at any rate, they wanted us then." With all the sufferings of those years, women had freedom and respect and money of their own. No one talked callously of unwanted women then.

*   *   *

171

VIRGINIA WOOLF, 1882 - 1941

Three Guineas, 1938

There is good reason to think that the word "Miss," however delicious its scent in the private house, has a certain odour attached to it in Whitehall which is disagreeable to the noses on the other side of the partition; and that it is likely that a name to which "Miss" is attached will, because of this odour, circle in the lower spheres where the salaries are small rather than mount to the higher spheres where the salaries are substantial. As for "Mrs.", it is a contaminated word; an obscene word. The less said about that word the better. Such is the smell of it, so rank does it stink in the nostrils of Whitehall, that Whitehall excludes it entirely. In Whitehall, as in heaven, there is neither marrying not giving in marriage.

"One sex remained inside"
Emily Brontë, for instance, who wrote
>   No coward soul is mine,
>   No trembler in the world's storm-troubled sphere;
>   I see Heaven's glories shine,
>   And faith shines equal, arming me from fear.
>
>   O God within my breast,
>   Almighty, ever-present Deity!
>   Life   that in me has rest,
>   As I - undying Life - have power in Thee!

though not worthy to be a priest in the Church of England, is the spiritual descendant of some ancient prophetess, who prophesied when prophecy was a voluntary and unpaid occupation. But when the Church became a profession, required special knowledge of its prophets and paid them for imparting it, one sex remained inside; the other was excluded. "The deacons rose in dignity - partly no doubt from their close association with the bishops - and become subordinate ministers of worship and of the sacraments; but the deaconess shared only in the preliminary stages of this evolution." How elementary that evolution has been is proved by the fact that in England in 1938 the salary of an archbishop is £15,000; the salary of a bishop is £10,000 and the salary of a dean is £3,000. But the salary of a deaconess is £150; and as for the "parish worker," who "is called upon to assist in almost every department of parish life," whose "work is exacting and often solitary . . ." she is paid from £120 to £150 a year; nor is there anything to surprise us in the statement that "prayer needs to be the very centre of her activities." Thus we might even go further than the Commissioners and say that the evolution of the deaconess is not merely "elementary," it is positively stunted; for though she is ordained, and "ordination . . . conveys an indelible character, and involves the obligation of lifelong service," she must remain outside the Church; and rank beneath the humblest curate.

*　　*　　*

CICELY HAMILTON, 1872 - 1952

The Englishwoman, 1940

England's advantages
If a woman is destined to go through life unwed, my country of England has many advantages as a domicile; there are, I imagine, few parts of the world where the once traditional contempt for the spinster is more thoroughly a thing of the past. Time was - and not so very long ago - when the middle-aged Englishwoman who had not found a husband was considered fair game for the jester; by the humorists of the Victorian age she was always depicted as a figure of fun - an unattractive creature who, in spite of all her efforts, had failed to induce a man to marry her. That was the old maid as a past generation saw her - and as we do not see her today; we have too many unmarried women successful in business or professional life, distinguished in literature, science, and art, to be able to keep up that joke.

*　　*　　*

VERA BRITTAIN, 1896 - 1970

Testament of Friendship, 1940

The views of Winifred Holtby, 1898 - 1935

"I might one day marry, simply because detachment *(sic)* is negative, and contacts, experiences and so forth, the stuff of life. I believe that life is intended to be corporate as well as individual - only I think with you that marriage is probably no more enchanting than any other great emotion . . .

The point is that I am a childless spinster and can make with ease an income of £1,000 a year if I *want* to make money. I was brought up economically and simply should not know how to spend all that on myself. At the moment, however, there is a good deal of family sickness up here in which all funds are welcome, and I am very glad indeed to have the £18 15s. 6d. to help pay for an aunt's operation."

"I am a feminist," she once wrote in the *Yorkshire Post*, "because I dislike everything that feminism implies. I desire an end of the whole business, the demands for equality, the suggestions of sex warfare, the very name of feminist. I want to be about the work in which my real interests lie, the study of inter-race relationships, the writing of novels and so forth. But while the inequality exists, while injustice is done and opportunity denied to the great majority of women, I shall have to be a feminist with the motto Equality First. And I shan't be happy till I get . . . a society in which sex-differentiation concerns those things alone which by the physical laws of nature it must govern, a society in which men and women work together for the good of all mankind, a society in which there is no respect of persons, either male or female, but a supreme regard for the importance of the human being. And when that dream is a reality they will say farewell to feminism, as to a disbanded but victorious army, with honour for its heroes, gratitude for its sacrifice, and profound relief that the hour for its necessity has passed."

*   *   *

174

T. S. ELIOT, 1888 - 1965

The Cocktail Party, 1943

Reilly: And this man. What does he now seem like, to you?

Celia: Like a child who has wandered into a forest
Playing with an imaginary playmate
And suddenly discovers he is only a child
Lost in a forest, wanting to go home.

Reilly: Compassion may be already a clue
Towards finding your own way out of the forest.

Celia: But even if I find my way out of the forest
I shall be left with the inconsolable memory
Of the treasure I went into the forest to find
And never found, and which was not there
And perhaps is not anywhere? But if not anywhere,
Why do I feel guilty at not having found it?

Reilly: Disillusion can become itself an illusion
If we rest in it.

Celia: I cannot argue.
It's not that I'm afraid of being hurt again:
Nothing again can either hurt or heal.
I have thought at moments that the ecstasy is real
Although those who experience it may have no reality.
For what happened is remembered like a dream
In which one is exalted by intensity of loving
In the spirit, a vibration of delight
Without desire, for desire is fulfilled
In the delight of loving. A state one does not know
When awake. But what, or whom I loved,
Or what in me was loving, I do not know,
And if that is all meaningless, I want to be cured
Of a craving for something I cannot find
And of the shame of never finding it.
Can you cure me?

Reilly: The condition is curable.
But the form of treatment must be your own choice:
I cannot choose for you. If that is what you wish,
I can reconcile you to the human condition,
The condition to which some who have gone as far as you
Have succeeded in returning. They may remember
The vision they have had, but they cease to regret it,
Maintain themselves by the common routine,
Learn to avoid excessive expectation,
Become tolerant of themselves and others,
Giving and taking, in the usual actions
What there is to give and take. They do not repine;
Are contented with the morning that separates
And with the evening that brings together
For casual talk before the fire
Two people who know they do not understand each other,
Breeding children whom they do not understand
And who will never understand them.

Celia: Is that the best life?

Reilly: It is a good life. Though you will not know how good
Till you come to the end. But you will want nothing else,
And the other life will be only like a book
You have read once, and lost. In a world of lunacy,
Violence, stupidity, greed . . . it is a good life.

Celia: I know I ought to be able to accept that
If I might still have it. Yet it leaves me cold.
Perhaps that's just a part of my illness,
But I feel it would be a kind of surrender -
No, not a surrender - more like a betrayal.
You see, I think I really had a vision of something
Though I don't know what it is. I don't want to forget it.
I want to live with it. I could do without everything,
Put up with anything, if I might cherish it.
In fact, I think it would really be dishonest
For me, now, to try to make a life with *any*body!
I couldn't give anyone the kind of love -
I wish I could - which belongs to that life.

Oh, I'm afraid this sounds like raving!
Or just cantankerousness . . . still,
If there's no other way . . . then I feel just hopeless.

Reilly: There *is* another way, if you have the courage.
The first I could describe in familiar terms
Because you have seen it, as we all have seen it,
Illustrated, more or less, in lives of those about us.
The second is unknown, and so requires faith -
The kind of faith that issues from despair.
The destination cannot be described;
You will know very little until you get there;
You will journey blind. But the way leads towards possession
Of what you have sought for in the wrong place.

Celia: That sounds like what I want. But what is my duty?

Reilly: Whichever way you choose will prescribe its own duty.

Celia: Which way is better?

Reilly: Neither way is better.
Both ways are necessary. It is also necessary
To make a choice between them.

Celia: Then I choose the second.

Reilly: It is a terrifying journey.

Celia: I am not frightened
But glad. I suppose it is a lonely way?

Reilly: No lonelier than the other. But those who take the other
Can forget their loneliness. You will not forget yours.
Each way means loneliness - and communion.
Both ways avoid the final desolation
Of solitude in the phantasmal world
Of imagination, shuffling memories and desires.

Celia: That is the hell I have been in.

177

Reilly: It isn't hell
Till you become incapable of anything else.
Now - do you feel quite sure?

Celia: I want your second way.
So what am I to do?

* * *

LESLIE D. WEATHERHEAD

In Quest of a Kingdom, 1943

I want you to imagine two young women in the early twenties.
They both want to be missionaries. They are both splendid
women, with fine physique, perfect health, radiant Christian
faith and splendid education, and they both go to a certain
Missionary Society. Their lives are before them, and they have
all their equipment and training in readiness. They are both
accepted. One goes to the Mission Field and spends her life as
she had planned to spend it, in magnificent service for Christ.
She marries a young missionary. She has her home, her
husband, her family and her work. One might say, she lives
happily ever after.
But the second, with the same health and qualifications and
the same determination, went back from the Committee which
had accepted her and sat for a long time alone in a room,
staring into the fire, and then she wrote a letter to the Committee, saying this: "I am very sorry, but I have changed my
mind and I am not free to go. I cannot leave two aged parents
who depend entirely on me". She meant life for them. At the
"eleventh hour" they passed away. But alas, for her also, the
day was now far spent. She put in an "hour" of her life in the
kind of work she wanted to do, but without the thrill, the
joyous, youthful giving, the splendid sacrifice. Missionary
activity at forty-seven in London isn't like going to India at
twenty-five.

* * *

MARGERY FRY, 1874 - 1958

The Single Woman, 1953

"The monotonous courage of years"
If this talk does nothing else, it gives me a chance of expressing admiration for the monotonous courage of years spent in caring for relatives sick or old for whose happiness and comfort many women barter their own lives, gladly enough perhaps when love prompts, often at the mere call of duty. But the giving and the taking of such help demands a graciousness that is not always kept up. . . .

The relative who accepts the gift of another person's life must respect as far as possible her limited freedom, her need for privacy and recreation. . . .

Her loving kindness will gain, not lose, from any independent life of her own she can maintain: she also has to guard against the martyred attitude, she also must lay up interests for the future. . . .

The art of "purring"
The art of "purring when you are pleased" does much to smooth the small asperities of life.

*   *   *

ESYLT NEWBERY

Parson's Daughter, 1958

"Something would remind me of Father!"
A friend of mine who was looking over what I have written here, said to me: "But haven't you ever been in love? Why don't you say something about it?"
In love! Of course I have, dozens and dozens of times, but unhappily, I invariably got tired of it first. For a bit it was always wonderful, and I was sure that this was the great romance of my life at last, and then something my admirer of

the moment said or did would remind me of Father! It would be all up! I could not go on with it! Heaven knows how hard I tried to conquer this sudden feeling of aversion, for I knew that I was sometimes giving real pain, and causing great unhappiness, also I longed for children of my own more than anything else in the world, and I believe that my restlessness, and mania for travelling, may have had its root in trying to smother this feeling of frustration.

But looking back, I know that I have had a happy life, eleven years with all three children, and nearly two more with Mike alone. Then again, it was a good life in Shanghai, and I think of the travelling, and wonderful interest of the different countries I have seen, since the children left. I've seen quite a large slice of the world, and lived fully and adventurously, and if I could have the time all over again I don't think I would want to change anything.

*　　*　　*

THE GUARDIAN, NOVEMBER 29, 1965

"Mainly for Women"

Mary Stott
Talking to spinsters

Once on this page I announced "I am no warped spinster waving the feminist flag," and thereby gravely offended some spinster readers. I was startled and wounded to think that anyone could have imagined I automatically equated "spinster" with "warped" but have always wanted to make amends. The moment has arrived. Already simmering over Professor Richard Selling's attack on "bitchiness, pettinesss, and lack of cooperation among matrons and senior doctors" (including men doctors, one presumes?), I was brought to the boil by reading that Richard Williams, a film cartoonist, said he had to leave his native Toronto because "They have the mentality of maiden aunts."

Dear spinsters, I rush, I fly to your defence. WHO runs the

180

"clean up television" campaigns? Not "maiden aunts," but the happily married mums. WHO is the bane of the serious theatre? Not "maiden aunts," but the tired business man with his preference for kicks and laughs. As a matter of fact there aren't any maiden aunts any more, living on cosy incomes from their fathers, or needing to ingratiate themselves into the homes of married brothers and sisters by being dimly useful and agreeable. Single women earn their living in the hard, hard world, and are less likely to wear blinkers than those who are well-cushioned by the security of family life.

But what about spinsters being "warped?" Perhaps living too much alone tends to make any human being odd. Self-centred, if not selfish, because there's no one who wants something different on the goggle-box, no one who loathes the smell of curry, no one who can't be cured of leaving soppy tea-towels crumpled on the draining board. Eccentric, sometimes, because there's no one to say "Are you going out in that hat?" or "The place for dogs to eat is in the kitchen." Clams, or more often, compulsive talkers, because there's no one to listen each evening to the tale of the day's small doings. Yet looking around my friends I can't think of any spinsters warped in these days. It is the elderly widows and widowers one worries over . . . and compulsive talkers tend to be wives housebound with young children, whose husbands are often away from home.

Bitchy spinsters? Useless to deny there are some, because envy, spite, malice, the desire to protect one's self-importance are common human failings. Possibly these failings are a special temptation for the unmarried woman if she still feels cheated of life's greatest good, a home, a husband and children, or feels despised for her failure to capture a man. Power over other people's lives can be a compensation for emptiness at the centre of one's own. But when spinsters become bosses are they all worse, more petty, more intolerant, more power-conscious than men? Well, are they? I don't know, for I never worked for a woman. I *have* worked for a few bitchy, napoleonic, pettifogging, or back-stabbing men.

Dear spinsters, don't sit down under these gibes. There is no reason for you to feel second-class citizens. You are not "surplus women" any more. You are the pearls beyond price, the frontline troops of the Welfare State; not only the people

181

who carry the organisational burden of the great hospitals, the great girls' schools, but the people who cherish the frail, dependent old, when married sisters and brothers can't find room for them in their tightly packed homes and lives. You are most desperately needed until society makes it easier for the married women to come along and help you to man the services their children need. You are only to be pitied if you pity yourselves.

But by and large spinsters are not a self-pitying lot, and they keep their burdens to themselves. They set up their attractive homes, often in amicable pairs, they travel abroad, they entertain delightfully and talk well. If they feel sexual deprivation, or if they decide to take love as and when they find it, or if they choose to be "the other woman," or if they are lesbians, they don't moan about it. Homosexual males deserve every intelligent person's support for reform of the outrageous law under which they suffer, but they deserve not one scrap more sympathy for their sexual loneliness than the spinsters - and widows - who cope with such courage and cheerfulness and make such good lives.

Dear spinsters, I salute you. Is this amends enough?

*　　*　　*

THE OBSERVER, JANUARY 23, 1966

Katharine Whitehorn

Living without Sex

In getting to the world's top female job, it seems to me that Indira Gandhi has a double edge in the competition. To start with she's a Nehru, which is always the most important thing about that family, overriding minor differences of sex and temperament; but she also has the advantage of being a widow, so that she need neither trip over her husband in the path of destiny nor be jeered at because she hasn't got one.

One would like to think, of course, that in this enlightened age the single woman had no social disadvantages to overcome. But I'm not sure things aren't getting worse in this respect and not better.

There are, for one thing, fewer and fewer of them. This is partly because there are more marriageable men around than before, partly because there's more money; but mainly because Freud and J. Walter Thompson between them have decreed that if you aren't successful at sex you aren't successful at anything.

Unbelievable

Sex, they say, must be the dominant drive in everybody's life. You would think that a casual glance at a busful of housewives - the Cabinet - the W1 - the Rotary - would make them think twice about the idea: do they *look* as if their lives were governed by sexual passion? Yet the single woman is supposed to be out of it just because hers can't be.

You can't be happy, it says here, without sexual fulfilment. These women *are* happy? Very well then, they are sleeping with their lapdogs, with Beelzebub, with each other. The generation that says we should strain our tolerance (not to say credulity) to include those who sleep with apes and peacocks apparently cannot take the idea of people who sleep with nobody: or even of people who would rather sleep with nobody than sleep with the wrong ape.

Honi soit. . .

One knows so well the incidental irritations of this viewpoint. You sit up half the night listening to the wails of some jilted bachelor, only to hear a casual bystander say, next day, that, so old and so unmarried, he must be queer. Not a psychological work that doesn't owlishly repeat that Lesbian couples are not frowned on in our society, since pairs of single women live openly together - rather missing the point that only those with absolutely one-track minds ever think they are Lesbians at all. I often wonder what the real Lesbians think about this unwarranted swelling of their ranks.

And a woman I know who has been interviewing a number of single women says she finds the ones under 40 are all nervously anxious to tell her about their sex life as soon as she gets in the door, for fear she should think they don't have one. What is so maddening about this tendency to see hormones in

183

stones, crooks in the running brooks and sex in everything is that it gets in the way of so many other human affections.

Just good friends

The great Victorian family may have harboured an occasional Mr. Barrett in its midst, but at least the rest could rely straightforwardly on having cousins and uncles to love at least. But for people who see Freud not only under every bed but under every desk and armchair as well, all friendly contacts patterned on *other* family relationships, on feelings of fathers for sons, mothers for anything weak, aunts for small nephews, sisters for sisters, become shrunk to this single idea.

The result of it can be that people on their own are cut off by sheer self-consciousness from a whole lot of deep human contacts - enough of which might make them scarcely notice that they *were* alone.

I suppose you could say that a woman who thinks she is better off single (or who simply finds herself single and makes a good job of it) shouldn't bother one way or the other what anyone thinks about it; but I think this is naive. People always are sustained or hurt by what others think of them.

No alternatives

The generation of splendid spinsters now nearing retiring age may have lived in single cussedness as far as general opinion was concerned; but the people who mattered to them thought of them as pioneers, as people proving something of value about woman's freedom; the wives in the bridge club may have thought they were missing something but at least the feeling was mutual. But of today's generation of girls well over 90 per cent will get married, which means in effect that they are growing up without a serious celibate alternative; which presumably goes (aren't mathematics wonderful) for the men, too. I think it's a pity.

Look at all those men who live for their work - all those wives (ask any social worker) whose attitude to sex is "My husband's very good - he doesn't bother me much"; the dedicated tea-cosy women who can shed light through a whole hostel of refugees; the men whose talent for domesticity, for giving a woman enough emotion to live on, is just about zero; what are we doing by making them feel they have to be hitched at all costs?

Of course, the theory is that we'll get psychology, chromo-somes, baby care and housing so streamlined that everyone will grow up a perfect mate - but is it likely?

In the Middle Ages, you could be a nun; in the last century a quarter of the population never got married at all; a number of advanced civilisations have got that way partly by offering to those who were better at something else an honoured alternative to mating. If ours is ceasing to do so, it will be the narrower for it. Pigeon-holing people is always a clumsy policy, especially if the hole has another pigeon in it already.

*   *   *

DAILY MAIL, SEPTEMBER 25, 1969

Stay A Spinster, Miss Whitehall, If You Want To Get To The Top

By Gordon Greig

If a woman wants to get to the top in Whitehall she usually has to give up the idea of marriage. Three out of five of the women who have become administrators, the elite class of Civil Servants who advise Ministers and influence policy, have stayed single.

But there has been no similar hesitation about marriage among the top men Civil Servants. Only one in ten has stayed a bachelor.

A report out yesterday on Civil Service recruiting methods says: "Progress into the higher grades of a class usually involves spinsterhood."

The Civil Service is described as a good employer of women. There is no sex discrimination over pay, promotion or holidays.

"Even so all the signs are that they compete on less than equal terms with men," says the report, which gives the results of a survey presented to the Fulton Committee inquiry into the Civil Service by Dr. A. H. Halsey, of Oxford University, and Mr. I.M. Crewe, of Lancaster University.

185

The Fulton findings were announced last June, but this is the first time the evidence has been published.

The report says that women are heavily concentrated in the lower grades although likely to be better qualified, at least in the formal sense, than men in the same grade.

Socially and educationally they are usually superior to the men who work alongside them.

But women form only 8 per cent of the administrative class, 9 per cent of the legal class and 20 per cent of the executives. They make up 44 per cent of all the clerks in the Civil Service.

One suggestion by the report - more flexible arrangements should be made to allow married women to return to work after their children have grown up.

*　　*　　*

THE TIMES, OCTOBER 3, 1969

Baroness Stocks

Extract from "The Modern Middle Class"

"And the majority of them were maiden aunts"
It is probably true that the social and administrative reforms of the nineteenth and twentieth centuries owe their existence almost entirely to the imagination, conscience and initiative of the middle classes. The working classes had neither the time nor the education to do much beyond the very considerable achievements of the co-operative movement, the friendly societies, and the trade unions, which were, of course, inspired by the self-interest of their class. But any student of social history will find its pages strewn with the names of financially well-endowed, middle-class leisured women. What names leap to mind? Florence Nightingale, Octavia Hill, Eleanor Rathbone, Emma Cons, Beatrice Webb, Margaret Frere, Rachel Macmillan, Margaret Llewelyn Davies, Emily Davies - one might run on. And the majority of them were maiden aunts. Only between 1905 and 1914 were their

186

energies diverted by the tedious and time-absorbing, but necessary, business of winning the vote.

Nor should the contributions of the domestic servants go un-recorded; for they were the "back room boys" of these fruitful activities. It was they who produced the leisure.

"The Lord giveth and the Lord taketh away." What has the social revolution done to the women of the middle classes? Balancing what has been given and what has been taken away, are middle class women disposed to add: "Blessed be the name of the Lord"? First and foremost it has taken away their freedom from domestic drudgery. It has taken away, or at any rate, seriously crippled the power of their bread-winning fathers to endow them with unearned incomes, As for the maiden aunts, they are now seldom maiden; and with the changing sex ratio of our population they are increasingly less likely to remain unsought in marriage.

*   *   *

WILLIAM HAMLING, M.P.
Vice President of the National Council for the Single Woman and her Dependants

Putting an Amendment at the Committee Stage of the 1971 Finance Bill, May 26, 1971

They have a right to work. They have a right to be independent. They have a right, for example, to pursue their careers. I can think of many school teachers, nurses and social workers, who have to care for elderly parents. These professional people should be able to follow their jobs. If we make it easier for them to do so, the taxpayer will benefit, because their incomes will provide revenue to the Treasury.

The continuance of people in employment would not only bring in more tax; it would also reduce the reliance of people on supplementary benefits. The State would get more revenue from tax and also would spend less on supplementary benefits. There are these complementary interests to both the Treasury and the Department of Health and Social Security, which the

Committee should bear in mind. Moreover, it is an unjust discrimination to accord tax relief where there are children, who might no longer be physically dependent, and to deny it where dependants are old or infirm. This is a claim in equity, as well as a claim on our sympathies and humanities. . . .

I often think that it is because they are women that their needs are not met. If they were men they would stand up and demand change. It is not in the nature of women to stand up and demand. They ask nicely. They are turned down nicely, but they are still turned down.

INDEX

References to authors are printed in Roman type and those to subjects in Italics.